Special Problems in Counseling the Chemically Dependent Adolescent

T0314695

Special Problems in Counseling the Chemically Dependent Adolescent

Eileen Smith Sweet
Editor

Routledge
Taylor & Francis Group

NEW YORK AND LONDON

First published in 1991 by Haworth Prees, Inc.,
10 Alice Street, Binghamton, NY 13904-1580

Published 2016 by Routledge
711 Third Avenue, New York, NY 10017
2 Park Square, Milton Park, Abingdon, Oxon OX14 4RN

Routledge is an imprint of the Taylor and Francis Group, an informa business

Special Problems in Counseling the Chemically Dependent Adolescent has also been published as *Journal of Adolescent Chemical Dependency,* Volume 1, Number 4 1991.

© 1991 by The Haworth Press, Inc. All rights reserved. No part of this work may be reproduced or utilized in any form or by any means, electronic or mechanical, including photocopying, microfilm and recording, or by any information storage and retrieval system, without permission in writing from the publisher.

Library of Congress Cataloging-in-Publication Data

Special problems in counseling the chemically dependent adolescent/ Eileen Smith Sweet, editor.
     p. cm
     "Has also been published as Journal of adolescent chemical dependency, volume 1, no. 4 1991" – T.p. verso.
     ISBN 1-56024-162-4 (alk. paper). – ISBN 1-56024-163-2 (pbk. :alk.paper)
     1. Teenagers – Drug use. 2. Drug abuse counseling. 3. Teenagers-Counseling of. 4. Compulsive behavior – Patients – Counseling of. I. Sweet, Eileen Smith.
     [DNLM: 1. Counseling – methods. 2. Substance Dependence – in adolescence. 3. Substance Dependence – rehabilitation. W1 J0533RL v. 1 no. 4 / WM 270 S7405]
RJ506.D78S64 1991
616.86'00835 – dc20
DNLM/DLC
for Library of Congress   91-20804
                                                                                          CIP

ISBN 13: 978-1-56024-163-8 (pbk)

This book is dedicated to Lila and Cinnie, in the hope that the world will be a better place for them.

Special Problems in Counseling the Chemically Dependent Adolescent

CONTENTS

ABOUT THE EDITOR

Eileen Smith Sweet, PhD, is a licensed psychologist and a certified addictions specialist. She directs the Addictions Studies Program at Montclair State College in Upper Montclair, New Jersey, where she is Assistant Professor in the Counseling Department. Dr. Sweet has published widely in the area of chemical dependency, adolescence, multicultural counseling and the family. She is on the Editorial Board of the *Journal of Adolescent Chemical Dependency* and has a private family therapy practice in Bogota, New Jersey, where she specializes in the treatment of addictions.

Foreword

Adolescence is a time of change and turbulence. Each individual experiences adolescence in a different and unique way, depending on the circumstances and the environment surrounding this period of development. Adolescence is the uncertain transition from childhood to adulthood with all the fears, feelings and change that dominate this developmental stage.

Adolescence is a struggle for independence counteracted by the fear of separation. The adolescent is pushing out of the nuclear family into a wider social world and at the same time resisting the separation and autonomy that results from this move towards independence. There is a fear of domination from parental control contrasted with a fear of abandonment and the feeling of insecurity about assuming responsibility for oneself. The need for autonomy is in conflict with the fear of abandonment.

Adolescents struggle with the desire to be unique, yet fear being seen as different from the norm. There is a strong need to belong and to be accepted by peers. Change is not easy for most people and it is especially difficult for the adolescent who is experiencing great change in a short time. This is a period to question values and separate from parents, which often results in an identity crisis. The support of family, teachers and peers is an important ingredient for any adolescent in order to cope with these changes without emotional, physical and social damage.

The use of drugs can so easily become the means for short term coping as well as a regulator of childhood memories. Drugs can become the way to handle the fear of abandonment and resistance to separation. Drugs can also be the means of coping with the desire for independence. If the adolescent is not able and willing to look within for identification and feelings of self-esteem, he or she is forced to externalize the struggle for control of feelings, and insight.

Treating adolescents with chemical dependency is a unique and challenging task. This population has problems which are distinctive to its developmental stage. Before the counselor begins the treatment process, it is imperative that there is awareness and understanding of the special needs that adolescents bring to treatment.

This book is an attempt to help the reader to better understand the dif-

© 1991 by The Haworth Press, Inc. All rights reserved.

ferent addictions that affect the adolescent population and the pertinent factors that complicate the treatment. There is discussion about the disease of chemical addiction, mental illness, child abuse, gambling, eating disorders and cults. These are discussed in relation to the identified teenage client as well as the total family structure of the client. There are also case studies and treatment suggestions which will help the reader to better grasp the complicated factors in adolescent chemical abuse and treatment.

Marian Schmidt, author of the article "Problems of Child Abuse with Adolescents in Chemically Dependent Families," uses the broad definition of child abuse which includes any act of aggression committed on a child that requires medical attention or causes concern for the wellbeing of the child. This definition includes so much more than the picture that most have of the "bruised, bleeding child." Physical abuse is only one aspect of child abuse. Abuse can and does also include emotional and sexual acts of omission and commission that are harmful to the child. Therefore incest is not only a physical sexual act, but encompasses exhibitionism, voyeurism, pornography and explicit language.

Schmidt reports that one half of all child abuse situations are related to alcohol use and abuse. Sixty percent of the families with an alcoholic member experience some type of domestic violence. With statistics this high it is evident that in the treatment of chemical dependency, child abuse is an important issue. Child abuse in a chemically abusing situation can range from fetal alcohol syndrome to the adolescent who has to take charge of his or her own life because of the absence of adequate supervision.

It becomes important that clinicians develop the awareness and ability to recognize abuse. Schmidt clarifies the teenage issues that become exacerbated in chemically-abusing families. Ethnic background can also be influential in determining the use and abuse of chemicals. Since there is a correlation between chemical use/abuse and child abuse, it is essential that clinicians are able to recognize these factors which point toward problem situations for adolescents and their families. She discusses the use of art therapy in the treatment of the abused adolescent. The Behavior Management-Artplay Program serves families who are at risk for child abuse because of domestic violence and/or substance abuse in their background. This unique therapy is successful in tension reduction between parents and children, resulting in better self expression, self esteem, and expression of feelings.

In the article, "Adolescence, Chemical Dependency and Pathological Gambling," William Pursley writes about the correlation between adolescent chemical use and gambling. He addresses the issues of dysfunctional homes, chemical dependency, and pathological gambling, giving insights into the nature of the problem and ways to deal with the problem.

During the developmental stage of adolescence there is a need for acceptance by both peers and adults. As the children move into adulthood by way of adolescence, they look for role models for behavior, values, morals and experience. It then is no surprise that chemical use and gambling become part of the journey to adulthood. Because adolescents are at the stage of developing their own set of values, behaviors and morals, they are vulnerable to all types of role modeling, peer pressure and impulses. There is a struggle to find out who they are apart from their parents, and at the same time to deal with the issue of self love. If the primary role modeling is from a dysfunctional home environment, there is evidence that the adolescent will adopt the same dysfunctional style. Children who receive the mixed messages and inconsistencies of dysfunctional parenting, suffer from confusion that leads to the distortion of self identification.

Pursley makes the connection of chemical use and abuse and pathological gambling based on the modeling afforded by the dysfunctional home environment. Because adolescents are vulnerable and easily influenced by the environment, their desire for immediate gratification and escape from pain leads toward pathological dependency. Pursley points out the commonalities of all addictive behaviors, including gambling. As the addiction repeats itself and worsens, it results in a greater need for relief and for denial of any problem. Because adolescents are in a developmental process at the same time that the addiction is developing, they tend to reinforce each other. The addiction becomes the means of supplying their needs. The behavior of addiction becomes the answer to the adolescents need for developing an identity, belonging, and physical expression. At the same time, the addiction provides a means of expressing autonomy from parental control. The addiction stops the natural developmental process of self identification, and shifts this to reliance on externals for identification. This results in distrust, fear, anger and low self-esteem.

Pursley suggests that the use of the cognitive behavioral modality is useful in helping the adolescents to recover from their addiction. The addiction is the primary focus of treatment which is also true in a twelve step model, so they can be blended together for optimum results. With the emphasis of our society on the externals of money, power, and fame, it is imperative that clinicians are aware of the increasing addiction of teenagers to chemicals, gambling and the combination of both. Because of the added complication of developmental changes in adolescence, it is important that the best treatment be available to those who are suffering the dual addiction of drugs and gambling.

Victor Stolberg and Dianne DeValve share their expertise in the field of chemical addiction and eating disorders in the article, "Eating Disorders and Chemical Dependency Among Students." These authors discuss anorexia nervosa, bulimia nervosa and compulsive eating, describing their commonalities of etiology with chemical addiction and the disease concept. The warning signs of eating disorders are given in a precise and orderly way for easy understanding and comprehension. Even though there is not a strong correlation found so far between eating disorders and chemical dependency in adolescents, there are many commonalities of etiology, treatment and assessment. Eating disorders seem to be on the increase in our society and affect adolescents with increasing frequency. An array of other problems, including chemical dependency are usually present among adolescents with eating disorders. Because eating disorders are not seen in a vacuum, it is important that clinicians are aware of the relationship with other problems including chemical dependency.

Adolescents are looking for an area of control in their lives: a sense of some autonomy. The need to become self reliant is strong and can manifest itself in the use of chemicals and/or control of eating habits which often results in an eating disorder. It becomes one area of life that can be controlled. Like chemical use, the compulsive use of food has certain pleasure inducing results, followed by a negative emotional state which is then motivation to compulsively seek the stimulus for pleasure. The repetition leads to addiction. The substance, whether it is food or other substances, is used to shut off feelings that cause emotional pain or to fill an emptiness. The adolescents who use any substance to meet an unfulfilled need have apparent personality similarities: poor boundaries, external controls, lack of discipline, lack of responsibility, self centeredness and grandiosity.

Stolberg and DeValve also share the results of a study done with students at a medium sized public eastern college. There was very little relationship found between eating disorders and chemical dependency in this study. The researchers, however, suggest that this does not eliminate any relationship, because the study was small and not representative of the total population. Additional research is needed to determine a relationship. The authors however, do find commonalities in treatment and assessment, which results in valuable practical suggestions for the reader. There is evidence that eating disorders and chemical dependency occur simultaneously in many cases, so it is essential that clinicians are knowledgeable about eating disorders.

Hans Gregorius and Thomas Smith provide the reader with an understanding of the relationship and effects of mental illness on the adolescent chemical abuser in his article, "The Adolescent Mentally Ill Chemical Abuser: Special Considerations in Dual Diagnosis." The treatment of the chemical abuser who also suffers from mental illness becomes complicated and recovery is less likely to be successful. If the adolescent has a preexisting mental illness, the use of chemicals has a synergistic effect or can produce a new illness. The adolescent who is already struggling with the natural turbulence in and incongruity of this developmental stage, the combination of chemical use and mental illness accelerates both diseases at a faster rate than the adult population. Adolescence, chemical abuse, and mental illness is a combination that results in a pathogenic mixture. Gregorius and Smith share their knowledge of dual diagnosis and insights into the treatment of adolescents with this diagnosis.

Because external dependency is so prevalent and powerful during adolescence, the process of mental illness and chemical dependency is speeded up during this stage. If the adolescent is a member of a dysfunctional family system, the process is even more accelerated and complicated. The dysfunctional family system does not encourage psychological growth, resulting in an enmeshed system in which the individuals look to external sources for identification and self esteem. Substances are often the external source for the adolescent to find some sort of peer identity and belonging as well as a means to cope. In turn if there is any form of mental illness, the disease of both substance abuse and mental illness are telescoped.

Gregorius and Smith share their knowledge about the consequences that substance use or abuse has on affective disorders, attention deficit disorder, learning disabilities, conduct disorder, antisocial disorder, and anxiety disorders. They also discuss the other psychiatric conditions that are affected by chemical use or abuse, elaborating on the added complication of these problems when found in the adolescent.

The reader is also given clinical implications for clients with dual diagnosis. There is not total agreement on the strategy for treatment, but most agree that the first goal is detoxification from the chemical before further evaluation and treatment of the mental illness. Gregorius and Smith's article makes very clear the necessity for clinicians to be aware of all the complications that may be present when treating the chemically dependent adolescent. It is imperative that counselors remain knowledgeable and have the resources available for treating all the different complicating problems that are present in adolescent development.

Peter Myers in "Cult and Cult-Like Pathways Out of Adolescent Addiction," shares his knowledge and insight into the attractions that cults can and do have for adolescents. Adolescents who are having difficulty coping with changes, pressures, and relationships are especially vulnerable to cults. Membership in a cult can be the answer to the desire to belong and be accepted. The adolescents who are already using or abusing drugs may find the total social network of the cult community a safe place from suffering. The recovering addicts also find the cult environment a place to belong and be accepted. The organization will also add structure to the unstructured life of addicts in recovery. The values and attitudes of the cult groups are an attraction to particular populations, including adolescents.

Adolescents may seek the cult to give predictability to their lives. The certainties of values and behavioral norms fulfill a need that adolescents are not finding in the family or peer group. It is a smaller social setting that is more manageable and less overwhelming than the association with the adult world. The cult supplies nurturing needs and develops a sense of community through support. It can also be a source of identity for adolescents who are finding it difficult to experience self identity.

Myers relates case studies that further clarify the correlation between chemical abuse and association with cults. He also includes an explanation of the different types of cults and their attraction to adolescents who have needs that are not being met within their own social setting. Myers discusses in depth the similarities and differences between a cult and support groups that recovering adolescents join, focusing mainly on Alcoholics Anonymous or other similar twelve step programs and the therapeutic community. The counselor needs to help the client be a full member of everyday society while still maintaining abstinence. The counselor must also be aware of the signs that the client in recovery may also be a member of a cult. The values and beliefs of the cult, whether political or religious will have an effect on the reaction of the client to treatment.

Paul B. Henry

Preface

It is only in the past thirty years that adolescents have been involved in the abuse of drugs to the level we see it today. Adolescence has always been a turbulent stage of development, but with the addition of chemical abuse it is even more confusing and stressful. It is important for the field of addiction studies to focus on the needs of this growing population. The treatment of adolescents with chemical addictions is complicated not only by the natural difficulties of this stage, but by external pressures and circumstances. The initial step to sobriety is only the beginning of therapy. The counselor must be aware of the all the needs of the adolescent to ensure the stability needed for abstinence.

Adolescence is a struggle between the desire for autonomy and the fear of being abandoned. Because of this stress, adolescents show a greater vulnerability for drug and alcohol use. Adolescence is a time to have a sense of identity as a unique person. Erik Erickson calls this a "who am I" period. The adolescent accomplishes the task of finding out who he is by experimentation with different lifestyles, resolutions of conflicts and rupture from childhood dependency. All adolescents have a need for power resulting from a lack of status, since they see themselves as neither child nor adult. There is also a common quest for autonomy, as reflected in individuality in fashion, hair style and language. There is a common desire for freedom of choice, yet a need for structure. There is a seeking for peer acceptance which is so strong that it sometimes overrides the adolescent's sense of morality, ethics and connection with the family. If any of these needs are not met, there is danger of the use of drugs to make up for the loss. Often the abuse of chemicals becomes the mode of coping and/or repressing needs. As the research demonstrates, the abuse of chemicals by adolescents is only a part of the total problem situation for many. Other problems such as eating disorders, gambling, cult membership and other compulsive behaviors often accompany the abuse of drugs. Without the adult role models that are necessary for successful passage into adulthood, the adolescent looks to a quick and easy answer to his or her needs. Because of the vulnerability and stress of adolescence, chemical use/abuse

© 1991 by The Haworth Press, Inc. All rights reserved. *xvii*

is an attractive alternative to dealing with the difficult realities of day to day living. Television programming and the importance put on external success by society teaches adolescents that gratification should be immediate. It becomes the expected way of life. Coping and problem solving skills are placed low on the priority list.

Child abuse is increasing in our society and needs to be considered when treating the adolescent with a chemical dependency. Child abuse can be physical, sexual, and/or emotional. A large percentage of the adolescents who abuse chemicals also have a history of some sort of abuse in the family. The use of chemicals often becomes the way to dull the reality of what is happening and the feelings that the abuse creates.

Mental illness among adolescents is also an area that needs more research and study. The adolescent who has a dual diagnosis of mental illness and chemical addiction has special treatment needs. The rehabilitation or habitation of the chemically addicted adolescent is a unique challenge and requires that the therapist is knowledgeable in the special problems, needs, and complications that go along with adolescence.

Dr. Eileen Smith Sweet has done an excellent job of collecting valuable information for all types of personnel who work with the adolescent population. *Special Problems in Counseling the Chemically Dependent Adolescent* is a collection of articles that are extremely useful for therapists, counselors, teachers, pastoral personnel, and parents who have contact with adolescents. The work is a concise and organized source of valuable information and treatment suggestions for this special population. The reader is given an explanation of the relationship between chemical dependency and other problems that are experienced by the adolescent who is trying to move from childhood into adulthood. The expertise of the different authors is shared with the reader for a better understanding of the developmental stage of adolescence and the complications that arise during this stage.

Paul B. Henry

Acknowledgements

Special acknowledgements to Megan Fernandez and Elaine Keeley for technical assistance afforded in the preparation of the manuscript.

What Do Adolescents Want?
What Do Adolescents Need?
Treating the Chronic Relapser

Eileen Smith Sweet

RELAPSE PREVENTION

Relapse prevention can be viewed in a number of different ways. One way is to look at what can be done differently to prevent a relapsed youngster from failing again. Another way to look at it, which will be discussed here, is to examine what important factors are involved, even before the problem of chemical dependency has appeared (Gorski, 1989).

CRISIS IN OUR SOCIETY

The largest place to begin world be with the world. A statement has been passed by the United Nations on the rights of the child — guaranteeing, among other things freedom from cruelty, freedom from want and the right to an education. It has been ratified by many nations of the world, but has yet to be ratified by the United States. A statement in support of the rights of the child on a national level would go far in helping to promote the goals of a psychologically healthy environment (Hart, 1990).

COMMUNITY SERVICE SYSTEMS

A concept, borrowed from cybernetics is useful here (Bateson, Jackson, Haley & Weakland, 1956). If one aspect of the prevention or educational feature of a treatment is neglected, it will weaken and cause other

Eileen Smith Sweet, PhD, directs the Addictions Studies Program at Montclair State College and is Assistant Professor in the Counseling Department. Specializing in addictions, she also has a private, family therapy practice located in Bogota, NJ.

© 1991 by The Haworth Press, Inc. All rights reserved.

1

areas to collapse. Yet, if multiple problems are treated simultaneously, the good effects from each will enhance and strengthen all of the other parts of treatment.

An environment which would discourage chemical abuse by our children would include affordable health care for all, including: the expectant mother, the unborn child, the infant and the elderly. Education which is freely available to all, including the single parent, would have ancillary supports, such as child care. Employment opportunities would be available for those well-trained individuals, who would receive child care and the provision of after school programs for their youngsters. An appropriate stipend would be available for those currently training for jobs through the private sector and community colleges, with a deadline for benefits, in which a job would be sought (Caplan, 1974).

PARENT TRAINING

Many families with chemically dependent children have not had positive models for child rearing (Gorski, 1984). Parent training could be offered through the staff of the local school systems, and would incorporate an alcohol and drug prevention and education component. Parents would be introduced to "whole health" concepts, which emphasize the ideas of "a natural high," nutritionally sound food, exercise and recreation.

This case study illustrates the use of both community systems and parent training.

> John, a twelve-year-old Black American was from a single parent home. His father was a cocaine addict and a compulsive gambler who abandoned his family when John was three years of age. As the sole means of support for her son and herself, it became necessary for John's mother to move to a poorer urban neighborhood. John was an only child and felt perpetually lonely, as though he didn't "belong" regardless of where he was, or whom he was with. Accompanying this persistent feeling was a deep-seated belief that he had been the cause of his father's departure, nine years earlier. By age eleven, John had joined a neighborhood gang, whose primary activity was smoking the drug crack cocaine. To gain acceptance, via "showing off" John began using crack quite often. After repeated problems in school and with storekeepers in his neighborhood, who accused John of stealing, the boy experienced heart pal-

pitations, and was brought to an area hospital's emergency room. Recognizing the effects of crack, hospital staff hospitalized John, and notified appropriate city agencies. The Division of Youth and Family Services became involved, with the result that John was committed to a short-term rehabilitation center for drug addiction. John returned home, and relapsed within half an hour. The boy's mother had absolutely no control over her son, and it was an obstacle which had been reinforced by her inconsistent disciplining of John throughout his life. However, after taking parenting training sessions through the school system, John's mother was able to set up house rules. Initially, John refused to follow his mother's mandates, and the boy was asked to move out. After spending another seven months vacillating between the streets and various institutions, John was invited back home. After a final relapse, John became sober, and has maintained his sobriety for over one year.

PEER COUNSELING AND MODELING

Some of the responsible students in upper elementary schools and high schools could be exposed to adventurous activities such as mountain climbing. Thus, these young people could taste a life that involves more courage and "healthy" risk-taking, while being protected against some of life's pitfalls, including the use of illicit drugs. Those so trained could bring this experience back to other students, and serve as models for them (Bandura, 1971).

As much praise and attention would be lavished on scholars, as is now bestowed upon athletes. Adolescents who achieve academically would serve as peer tutors. Furthermore, those students who were leaders in other areas, and exhibited the qualities of reliability and responsibility would be invited to offer peer counseling to their contemporaries.

PUBLIC RELATIONS AND MARKETING

One problem with the ideal models presented here is that they appear unappealing to youngsters who have been sold by the media on ideas of money, power, fame and prestige. The current symbol of success to today's adolescents always includes chemical use. Some large companies have begun to get involved in the marketing of whole health ideas, and have provided resources to schools and communities to glamorize, popularize and to promote the ideals of a healthy, chemically-free lifestyle (Scipione, personal communication 1. 28. 91).

THE CRIMINAL JUSTICE SYSTEM

A well educated and trained criminal justice system is mandatory if an end to the current crisis situation is desired. Personnel including judges, police and probation counselors must have thorough training in the prevention of drug abuse, as well as an extensive education on addictions. Obviously, in order for the system to function well, laws must exist that "have teeth in them." It is equally important that better educational and vocational opportunities are provided for the inmates in correctional institutions, so that these programs have a chance to really work (Linne, 1984).

APPROPRIATE SERVICES AND PERSONNEL

Insufficient adolescent treatment centers for drug and alcohol rehabilitation is another problem of crisis proportions. There are too few spaces in mental health centers, and the same holds true for all chemical abuse facilities. What is available does not always comprise the necessary components of choices to achieve recovery. This partnership has to include at the very least, the following:

1. A fully staffed detoxification unit (including twenty-four hour presence of medical doctors and registered nurses);
2. Inpatient programs — including long-term rehabilitation units, halfway houses and mental health facilities that deal with people who have been given a dual diagnosis;
3. Aftercare programs that require consistent attendance and often family involvement.

Training of personnel must be expanded to include special problems not included in most curricula, at this point in time. It is important that alcohol and drug staff for adolescent treatment in schools and facilities have, at the very least, training that is equivalent to that of other counselors in the fields of social work and psychology. Otherwise, these professionals will have an extremely difficult time commanding the respect that is appropriate for their positions, and that is necessary for the success of their work. No counselor of any kind should practice without preparation in multicultural counseling (Sandahl, 1984). Family systems therapy has become a "must" in intervention, especially with recalcitrant teenage relapsers. An extensive grasp of the family dynamics, often found in the chemically abusing home, is integral to success (Weidman, 1987). The counselor must learn to (and is expected to) recognize the "other" high risk factors (Marlatt & Friedman, 1981) in the families they are treating. Common red-flag problems are parental addictive issues, and dual illnesses on the part of the adolescent—such as psychiatric disorders, gambling and food disorders. The substance abuse counselor working with the teenager must also learn differential counseling techniques (Rud & Magee, 1986). One takes a very different approach with the chronic adolescent cocaine crack user, as compared with an adolescent who is newly involved in the addiction of alcoholism.

Other important criteria for staff would include staff members with the ability to make a differential diagnosis. All counselors would have a thorough grasp of intake, screening, treatment planning and referral skills.

This next case study provides an illustration of the systems approach and use of the differential diagnosis.

> Luanna is a 15-year-old Cuban-American high school student. She began experimenting with alcohol and drugs at the age of 13, and developed a pattern of turning to alcohol, in particular, when she felt depressed. Luanna's mother, an alcoholic, also struggled with depression, and dealt with her lengthy periods of melancholia with heavy alcohol consumption. Luanna noticed after a few months that whenever she picked up a drink while depressed, the depression became magnified, once she became drunk. Turning to cocaine, to combat the depression, Luanna eventually began having difficulty sleeping and became addicted to barbiturates also, to help her sleep. Luanna's parents became aware of their daughter's problem, and committed her to a long term rehabilitation center (a six month program). After her release from the institution, Luanna relapsed repeatedly. An alcoholism counselor at the girl's school suspected that Luanna's problems were more severe than were those of other adolescent drug addicts. Upon the counselor's recommendation, Luanna was sent to a psychiatrist, who was very sophisticated in regard to chemical dependency. The doctor diagnosed Luanna as suffering from a bipolar disorder as well as drug addiction. Since then, Luanna has been taking the drug lithium, and has achieved

more balance with her mood swings, while maintaining her sobriety for over ten months.

TRAINING CONSIDERATIONS

The Specifics of a Relapse Prevention Program

It is important that adolescent relapsers have a longer stay in institutions, than is currently practiced. That is, at least six months to a year is the minimum amount of time that programs need to invest in addicts, if any success is to be achieved. All aspects of counseling must be included: individual, group and family therapy sessions. A well thought out aftercare program, in which visits are gradually more widely spaced, is an integral aspect of a successful program. Every adolescent aftercare facility should offer access to the following self-help groups, on a permanent basis: a parents group, ACOA, AA, Al-Anon, NA and Naranon. This is the only method that ensures that a recovering teenager and his or her family will enjoy permanent continuity of treatment, and a long lasting support community.

Regarding family treatment, if there are no family members or significant others at the outset, an effort will be made to find surrogates, (e.g., people at 12-Step meetings, or long estranged relatives).

Specific Guidelines for Trainers

With the counselor of the relapse prone adolescent, it is important for the trainer to emphasize specific counselor characteristics. Clinicians must be sensitive while at the same time engaging in consistent honest communication with clients. This is not the population upon which to practice bravado confrontation techniques. Time and care are necessary to develop trust and to forge a strong therapeutic alliance. Therapy for the counselor, as well as weekly supervision are musts, to effectively deal with transference and countertransference manifestations. The "good mother" concept (Mahler, 1961) is applicable here; persistence and patience pays off. Interventions regarding problems of family members other than the identified client will be supplied (Cohen, 1989). It is vital that the counselor who works with adolescents possesses a thorough grounding in academic learning problems. This encompasses obtaining help for the youngster for any school problems, and providing ways to help the teenager to enhance his or her self concept (Myers & Brown, 1990). Counselors might also try a ploy that has been successful for this clinician:

Send an adolescent in denial to the *opposite* self-help program from that which is called for. Sending an addicted teenager to Alanon or Naranon, for example allows the addict to learn and understand far more about his or her own disease — from the perspective of non-addicted experts. Those who interact with addicts regularly and who experience negative contact with addicts, present an undiluted appraisal of the alcoholic/drug-addict that the addict would never be capable of reaching by him or herself.

The role of family treatment cannot be emphasized too strongly in combatting relapse. The following account illustrates the use of family systems.

> David, a fifteen year old Irish-American teenager, is worried about his parents. Until recently, he had been very close to his mother. Now in his teens, he is virtually ignored by his mother, who is engaged in an obsessive, codependent relationship with David's alcoholic father. Beginning to drink and use marijuana for the past few months, the boy has been getting into trouble in school. After repeated incidents, David was sent to an inpatient program at a rehabilitation center specializing in drug addiction. Upon his discharge, David immediately returned to drug and alcohol consumption. After a short time, and at the urging of the boy's high school guidance counselor, David's parents became involved in weekly family therapy sessions with David. During the sessions, the entire family was shown exactly how they had been expressing themselves and how they had been communicating with one another. It was pointed out that David in particular had been working diligently at accomplishing two things: First, David was single-handedly keeping his parent's marriage together; second, the boy was gradually increasing his self-destructive behavior, to garner more attention from his mother. Eventually, after being involved in treatment consistently, David's father became motivated by his son's concern and sought treatment for his own alcoholism. Today, David's father is sober and regularly attends A.A. meetings. The wife and mother in this family was the most motivated person. She became less obsessed with her husband's problems, and therefore had more emotional energy to give to David. A marked improvement took place in their relationship and the two related with each other in a healthier manner than they had before treatment. After a final relapse, David was able to remain sober, and has been sober for over three years.

The Place of Altruism

Of paramount importance in all of this discussion is the issue of restoring faith and hope to alienated adolescents. The most elegant way to do this is to encourage the practice of altruism. This will help youngsters to develop a sense of competence and simultaneously raise their self-esteem. It is wonderful to witness the joy that troubled teenagers express, after their lives have improved, and they are capable of helping others in significant ways.

REFERENCES

Bandura, A. (1971). *Psychological Modeling: Conflicting Theories*. Chicago: Aldine & Atherton.

Bateson, G., Jackson, D. D., Haley, J. & Weakland, J. H. (1956). Toward a theory of schizophrenia. *Behavioral Science*, 251-264.

Caplan, G. (1974). *Support Systems and Community Mental Health*. New York: Behavioral Publications.

Cohen, P. R. (1989). Promoting recovery and preventing relapse in chemically dependent adolescents. *Journal of Chemical Dependence and Treatment. 2* (No. 1): 205-238.

Gorski, T. T. (1989). Relapse — issues and answers. Alcoholism and Addiction. *Recovery Life* p. 21, Nov.

Hart, S. (1990). The Rights of The Child. Presentation at ISPA July, Newport: Rhode Island.

Linne, G. T. (1984). The impact of structural family therapy on the recidivism rate of adolescents arrested for substance abuse. 167 pp. PhD dissertation, United States International University (University Microfilms No. DA8420110).

Mahler, M. S. (1961). On sadness and grief in infancy and childhood: Loss and restoration of the symbiotic love object. *Psychoanalytic Study of the Child. 16*, 332-351.

Marlatt, G. A. and Friedman, L. F. (1988). Determinants of relapse: implications for treatment. Pp. 1183-1191. In: Schecter, A. J., ed. *Drug Dependence and Alcoholism*.

Myers, M. G. and Brown, S. A. (1990). Coping responses and relapse among adolescent substance abusers. *Journal of Substance Abuse. 2*: 177-189.

Rud, R. C. and Magee, K. (1986). Relapse prevention through treatment of primary depression in alcoholic patients: an exploratory study. P. 200. In: International Council on Alcohol and Addictions. International Institute on the Prevention and Treatment of Alcoholism. 32nd. (Abstracts/Resumes). 253 pp. Budapest, Hungary.

Sandahl, C. Determinants of relapse among alcoholics: a cross cultural replication study. *International Journal of Addictions 19*: 833-848.

Weidman, A. (1987). Family therapy and reductions in treatment dropout in a residential therapeutic community for chemically dependent adolescents. *Journal of Substance Abuse and Treatment. 4*: 21-28.

Problems of Child Abuse with Adolescents in Chemically Dependent Families

Marian G. Schmidt

INTRODUCTION

Initially, the current state of the field will be described with respect to abuse of adolescents in chemically dependent families. Findings and pertinent factors relating to the issue will be presented, as well as treatment approaches to it. Case examples will demonstrate a variety of treatment issues with abused and abusing adolescents. Finally, prevention measures will be considered.

DEFINING ABUSE

Child abuse has been defined as "an act of aggression that has been committed to the child which may require medical attention or create concern for the child's wellbeing" (Bavolek & Henderson, 1989); abuse of children has taken on a broad definition in recent years. Now that incidents such as exhibitionism with minors must be reported to state agencies, the image of the bruised, bleeding child is joined by the image of the silently suffering child who has been impacted in non-physical ways, or the unduly aggressive child who is reacting to the environment. Violence between adults may be said to be abusive to children, if they are present. Physically, emotionally, or sexually harmful acts of commission or omission, with severe emotional neglect can be just as damaging as physical abuse (Flanzer, 1982).

Incest is most commonly thought of where adolescent abuse is concerned; this may not necessarily involve physical contact in cases of exhi-

Marian G. Schmidt, PhD, is Staff Psychologist, Verona Counseling Center, Verona, NJ. Dr. Schmidt is in private practice, Upper Montclair, NJ.

© 1991 by The Haworth Press, Inc. All rights reserved.

bitionism, observation of the adolescent (voyeurism), pornography, or explicit language. There are a variety of types of "dry intercourse," and many kinds of unnatural restraint which constitute molestation (Sgroi, 1982).

About half of all abuse incidents are said to be related to alcohol alone (Finkelhor, Gelles, Hotaling, & Straus, 1983), and it is estimated that 60% of families with an alcoholic member experience domestic violence (National Council on Alcohol). Chemical abuse is known to be of many kinds, with hundreds of mood-altering substances available. Aggression is most clearly evidenced following use of ethanol, phencyclidine (PCP), amphetamines, and cocaine, whether it be during intoxication, withdrawal, drug-induced psychotic state, idiosyncratic behavior under normally benign circumstances, or secondary to the pursuit of money for the substance (Miller & Potter-Efron, 1990).

Psychoactive substance abuse is defined by the problems it generates, the danger of the problems, and their persistence (DSM III R, 1987). The adolescent who inhabits a family setting which includes chemical abuse is de facto at risk for child abuse by reason of the problems inherent in the life of the chemical abuser (which will be dealt with further below). Whatever may happen to the physiology, mood, or personality of the chemical abuser, the adolescent must fall into a pathologically assigned role (Barnard, 1984). Black (1982), using Adler's typology, has delineated some of the roles adopted by children of alcoholics. The young adolescent in an alcoholic family becomes designated by the dynamics of the family to act as "adjustor," "placator," or "the responsible one." In these roles emotional or other abuse takes place which eventually produces the adjustment problems of the adult child.

Just as chemical abuse may be episodic or steady in nature, the abuse of an adolescent may be a one-time incident, or an ongoing state of affairs, ranging from the effects of fetal alcohol syndrome, to an attraction for negative attention in relationships. The latter attribute applies especially to the incest victim, who may come to view him/herself as a sexual object with no rights to privacy, but it can also apply to the adolescent who has taken charge of his or her own life through absence of adequate supervision.

IDENTIFYING ABUSE IN ADOLESCENTS

Physical abuse of adolescents is unlikely to feature the fractures, burns, and internal injuries, which are common indicators in young children;

more likely are unexplained bruises, facial damage, and/or swollen or tender limbs (Bavolek & Henderson, 1989). A list of common indicators for sexual abuse is given by Bavolek & Henderson (1989), including: (1) apparent pain in sitting or walking, (2) pregnancy, (3) direct report from the child, (4) distorted body image, such as feelings of low self-esteem, shame, ugliness, self-depreciating, and self-punishing, (5) sex play with peers or objects, (6) drug use/abuse for blurring guilt and anxiety, (7) indirect allusion, such as wishing to live elsewhere, (8) seductive behaviors towards peers or adults.

Delinquent behaviors are often a sign of previous emotional abuse of adolescents. Defiance, rebellion, and incorrigibility may begin with refusal to observe rules at school and at home, and end with criminal acting out behaviors. The pseudomaturity of the adolescent who feels no one is in charge is often seen in cases of runaways, teenage pregnancy, and vandalism. In treatment these children reveal feelings of worthlessness, defeat, and depression.

DOCUMENTING THE ABUSE

While there is scant information in the child abuse literature on abuse of adolescents, other than incest, (Flanzer, 1990), the connection between chemical dependency and child abuse is well documented (e.g., Ackerman, 1987; Barnard, 1984; Bepko & Krestan, 1985; Bradshaw, 1988; Buckley, McCarthy, Norman & Quaranta, 1977; Cavaiola, 1989; Glynn & Haenlein, 1988; Nakken, 1988; Potter-Efron, 1990; Selekman, 1989; Smith, 1990); however, no figures have been provided by studies that directly link actual abuse and neglect of children with their parent's substance abuse (American Bar Association, 1986).

Adolescents constitute more than a fourth of abuse and neglect cases; about half of these are thought to be "graduates" of long-term abuse (Gabarino & Gabarino, 1987). (The National Committee for Prevention of Child Abuse gives total figures for reported child abuse and neglect reports of 2.4 million for the nation in 1989.) Reviews of adolescent chemical dependency treatment populations have found in one program 28% of 250 cases had been physically abused, and 9% had been sexually abused (Potter-Efron & Potter-Efron, 1985), while 30% of 500 cases in another survey were found to have been physically and/or sexually abused (Cavaiola & Schiff, 1988). According to Trepper and Barrett (1989), substance abuse precedes incest in the majority of cases.

PERTINENT FACTORS
IN ABUSE OF ADOLESCENTS

Barnard (1984) identifies the similarities between alcoholic and incestuous families as (1) blurred generational boundaries where the irresponsible parent adopts the child's level; (2) a disintegrating marriage where the parents can't team and the child becomes a surrogate spouse or is parentified; (3) diminishing sex in the marriage, with guilt and shame blurred by chemical abuse; (4) inhibition of normal anxiety, so that old anger spills over on the vulnerable child; (5) a muffled, distorted affect with a brittle lack of self-expression; (6) denial, secrecy and isolation, which reduce relatedness inside and outside the family; (7) rigid roles, with the child often in the adult role; (8) a sense of "stuckness," or rigid homeostasis, in which the abuse of the chemical or the child reduces family tension and thus maintains the pattern; (9) disturbed sibling relationships, with one child chosen as "special"; (10) an excess of belonging or separateness, so the child is smothered or alienated; (11) an absence of trust with corresponding failure to invest in emotional attachments; (12) a symbiotic dependence in which family members cannot function well interdependently. A problem for the clinician is the task of inducing the chemical abuser to acknowledge a lack of control over the use of the substance, while at the same time gain control of the child abuse.

Clinicians can recognize certain "red flags" which alert them to the possibility of detecting abuse with an adolescent, such as a poor mother-daughter connection, the presence of an alcoholic stepfather, sexual problems in the alcoholic marriage, use of corporal punishment in the background, a very dependent mother, a father who is jealous and controlling of the adolescent, a pseudomature, parentified, acting out adolescent, who may abuse chemicals to blur his or her own shame (Barnard, 1984).

Usual teenage issues become exacerbated in cases of chemically-abusing families. The generation gap in which many adolescents rebel in order to achieve healthy separation from their parents, in the case of an abused adolescent may lead to truancy, running away, delinquency, substance abuse, or violence towards parents. The normal attraction to members of the same or opposite sex may, instead, bring about promiscuity, prostitution, or victimization of younger children. Mood fluctuations which seem normal in the adolescent stage may, in these cases of abuse, indicate a more serious depression, because of the loss of confidence and sense of self-worth at a time when independent behavior is supposed to increase. A review by Smith (1990) of teenage suicide studies found more male teen-agers completed suicide, but without strong effects for the variables of substance abuse in the adolescent or in the family; females, on the other hand, made more suicide attempts and showed both a tendency to chemi-cal abuse and a background of physical or sexual abuse.

Emotional abuse is defined by the National Center on Child Abuse and Neglect as child abuse which impairs the psychological growth and devel-opment of the child. Gabarino and Gabarino (1986) identify five causes of emotional maltreatment of adolescents: (1) rejection, in which the child is infantilized, criticized harshly, or expelled from the family; (2) terroriz-ing, such as threatening to expose humiliating behavior (like enuresis); (3) ignoring the child, who is replaced by other objects of affection; (4) isolating the child by preventing from age-appropriate activities; (5) cor-rupting by involvement in deviant behavior. For those who have been shamed, power and control are sought to prevent further shaming. Thus the parent who has been shamed does to the child what the parents did to them — a reenactment of their own victimization in the revengeful position of offender (Bradshaw, 1988).

The ethnic background of the family can be influential in determining the course of use/abuse of alcohol in a family, and alcohol is known to be a gateway to the use of other substances. Coombs (1988) has looked into the various cultures that either promote the use of alcohol to enhance a sense of freedom, responsibility, and ethnicity (Irish, Mexicans, Polish) or control it for religious reasons (Jews, Italians, WASPs). If the adoles-cent moves towards the values of a peer group and away from the family traditions, the discrepancy in parent/child expectations may bring about substance abuse and violence on either level or both.

TREATMENT ISSUES

Primary care for adolescents seeks to prevent abuse on an outpatient basis. The young person seeks help from a trusted adult in the school or elsewhere, or is brought to a professional by a parent. The "problem" is usually an issue of autonomy, privileges, rebellion, and social control, with an inappropriate balance of nurturance and discipline on the part of the parents — corporal punishment getting out of hand, or else the adoles-cent taking charge of the parent(s). Referral may be made to a support group, such as Alateen, in order to provide peer support while education about substance abuse is delivered.

Secondary treatment stresses a mental health, rather than substance abuse, concept of the adolescent's problem. While education about substance abuse is still required, counseling should focus on self-development and should include the parent(s) from time to time, when a trusting relationship has been established. Informal or formal assessment of anxiety and depression should be ongoing. In the case of incest, Trepper and Barrett (1989) have outlined a course of treatment designed to reintroduce the offender into the family. Incest survivor groups for adolescents are becoming available, especially in hospital settings.

Tertiary, or inpatient treatment, assumes a high level of disability owing to multiple problems for the adolescent. Whether in a rehabilitation setting or a hospital ward, some adolescents are removed far from their homes to prevent the temptation to run away, while others need their families close at hand for support or therapy. Schooling must be provided to assure further intellectual development and reintroduction into the educational mainstream. Intense psychotherapy is usual with support personnel available on a 24-hour basis. The inpatient setting often provides the adolescent with the first "safe place" to unburden the pain of the exploited vulnerable person, betrayed by those who were depended upon. The inpatient setting often provides the adolescent with the first "safe place" to unburden the pain of the exploited vulnerable person, betrayed by those who were depended upon and by the disease of chemical dependency.

In the following cases the acronym COA for "child of an alcoholic" will be used to denote an adolescent whose parent was chemically dependent. Cases will exemplify COAs who have been abused, have abused others, and have abused substances.

THE ABUSED COA

In a large Irish-American family the father suffered an unaddressed alcohol problem. His wife, after rearing eight children, took a job and was glad to go to bed early, leaving him to his own company in the evening. He chose their middle daughter for a companion and when intoxicated, would rouse her from her bed and rage at her endlessly into the night. At other times he would set her above the other children, giving her special favors and approval. When she reached her teens, he began taking her on his lap to masturbate against her back; she was unwilling but afraid to deny him. He would also expose himself and masturbate, while requiring her to watch him. In her shame and distress she told no one, fearing blame for her special position with her father. At school she began a series of relationships that involved sexual subjugation which lasted through college. Not until after her marriage to a cool and sexually repressed man did she discover that her father had also made overtures to both of her older sisters, who rejected him. The natural reserve of the Irish family then broke; the siblings wept together and formed a team in support of each other.

Selekman (1989) explains how family members become stuck or restrained with each other after a vicious cycle of interaction has followed the mishandling of a problematic situation. In the case cited above, denial, isolation and secrecy were the norm: the father's alcoholism was tacitly considered an Irishman's prerogative and was never openly discussed. The parents' experienced isolation in their marriage and instituted it in their children, who could not confide in each other. When the middle daughter was "triangled" into the marriage by her father, she was scapegoated by her siblings as the special one, and had to resort to secrecy about her own part of the cycle. When she found herself overly angry with her first child, she sought therapy to break the cycle and simultaneously opened the door of confession and communication with her siblings.

THE COA WHO IS CHEMICALLY DEPENDENT

When she was nine, Mary began sipping beer with her third grade friends after school in the park. Her mother, who had divorced Mary's alcoholic father, came home from work at six; she had given up on after-school babysitters when Mary was eight. Mary spent school vacations coloring with crayons and watching television until her mother came home. The school made a report of suspected neglect, but Mary's mother was able to satisfy the authorities that her supervision of the child was adequate. Mary's mother bought wine by the gallon which she consumed alone at night, but she denied any problem with alcohol, because she never went over two gallons a week. Mary's father lived in the next town; she didn't like to visit him, because she missed her friends and because he "yelled" at her. One time she called her mother to fetch her from her father's house. Her mother worried that Mary might have been molested and brought her to counseling. Mary willingly discussed her relationship with beer, and denied any other substance abuse or mishandling by her father. Her mother made a decision to adopt complete sobriety and joined a parent support group. In the group she said:

Anyway they say to me, you should really take her on a Saturday and do something with her—usually I do, but it's like, that's my time . . . and I work Saturday night, so in fact the only night I have to do what I want is Friday night, and part of me really doesn't want to give up that Friday night, I mean I need that Friday at the end of the week. I feel so guilty about . . . I mean, sometimes she'll fight and "I don't want to go to Daddy" and I feel guilty about sending her, you know I say to her "I want you to go because I think it's important for you to have a relationship with him, no matter what he is," and she knows what he's like and really doesn't like going; I still think it's important, because I never knew my father until I was thirteen. But I feel immensely guilty sometimes making her go; I mean she could stay home with me, I'm not doing anything, but by Friday I'm reeling from—twenty-four hours a day just the two of us. I really really a lot of times need to have her away from me and out of my life for a while and not have to worry about it or think about it—I know she's safe, I know she's OK up there, she's being fed and everything's OK, but I really feel very guilty about it. And it's like, when does there become time for yourself when you don't feel guilty?

The conflict in a single parent between wanting and not wanting the responsibility for a child is common. The ambivalence in the parent can be validated, without giving permission for neglect. When resources can be found for the parent, the child will profit, but first the safety of the child must be assured. In the above case a method called "investigative interviewing" (Holman, 1983) was employed to assess the probability of neglect or abuse. Sensitive, focussed questions tracked Mary's behavior with her father and friends. Tools, such as a genogram of the family relationships and a "Pattern of Use Survey" of each member's history with alcohol and other chemicals led the way to discussions and decisions relating to the need for sobriety and increased supervision of the child.

THE ABUSIVE COA

Mark was the only son of parents who both abused a variety of chemicals. While his mother favored his two younger sisters, Mark was the apple of his father's eye. Favoritism grew to where Mark's mother resented his alliance with his father and the hint of macho superiority the boy seemed to imitate. When his father was "under the weather," he put

Mark in charge of the girls; their complaints were ignored if Mark was rough. Elsewhere Mark exhibited the same general air of omnipotence, until in high school he was remanded to the court for vicious fighting and molesting of younger children. His parents reluctantly accompanied him to mandated counseling from which his father soon withdrew. His mother persevered in attending and responded to a task set by the counselor to write an autobiographical history of her abuse of Mark (*sic.*):

> It started out as verbal abuse. I use to call you names, swearing and holling and I was pushing you away. I thought that your father thought that you did nothing wrong. That went on a while, then it went to physically. Verbal abuse started when you was about the age of six, that went on for about two years, then I started slapping you on the face, your arm, back and bottom. I use to kick you to just to get your attition or just stick my foot out to trip you. When I lose control of my actions I feel that I can't do anything right to please anyone. I felt that everyone just uses me to be there when they want something done. When I get really upset I feel like just taking off and leaving everyone. I feel like nobody will care if I am here or not. I just feel that nobody really loves me. I just want to run away. I hate myself. I know that it is all my fault for the abuse. It isn't yours. That was the only way that I knew how to handle it. That is the way that I was showed. That is how my mother used to punish my brothers and sisters and me. I don't know any other way to do it. Mark, I think that my violence has really bothered you. It has effected you more then you want to amit. I know that now when you get in a fight or you are mean to the (unreadable) ones at school that you are really trying to get at me. You probely want to really beat on me sometimes when you get angry because I have hurt you a lot . . . When I stop and think about it you really have the right to be mad or angry with me. But I am trying to change. Please help me. Mark, I am trying to tell you that I am sorry about the way that I have treated you. I know sometimes I don't act like a mother, but I am going to try harder. I was never tought how to be a mother or how to handle things like this. My mother wasn't home much to show me how to handle things, so I had to learn the hard way by my mastakes. I just want to tell you again I am sorry and I love you. Please give me a chance to show you that I am trying to change. I want to tell you again I love you and I want to try to start a new beginning.

The hostility aroused in a child by abuse may in some cases be relieved by molestation of younger or weaker children (Sanford, 1980). The relief of stress in this way may be so impelling that adolescents of good reputation are sometimes tempted into molestation of small children when babysitting them, etc. In Mark's case, a negative fusion between himself and his mother was the outcome of a family projection process in which males were accorded a more powerful stance over females, and females were validated in their anger at males. Crumbley (1985) notes that the child's demands may recall the parent's own anxieties and unmet needs, making the parent feel inadequate and unable to respond empathically. The goal of counseling following the mother's apology was to restructure the family towards a clear executive parenting team without role reversal (by uniting the parents) and negotiating dyadic relationships so that the boy has the same degree of differentiation from his mother as from his father.

THE ABUSED COA
WHO IS CHEMICALLY DEPENDENT

Fred and Cathy brought their 14-year-old Sandra to counseling because of poor school grades and defiance of home rules. Fred was in recovery from polydrug abuse; Cathy was a compulsively clean housekeeper who turned to a fundamentalist religion for support when her husband first became unfaithful and left the household. Their only child, Sandra, was in extreme distress because, as she told the counselor, she had always been able to get her father on her side against her mother, but now the two were teaming up against her. She confessed an earlier suicide attempt with pills, which passed unnoticed when she slept off the effects. She detailed a history of inappropriate punishment at the hands of her father and failure to win her mother's approval. Before the parents could be informed of the suicidal gesture, Sandra ran away and managed to support herself in another state for several weeks before returning voluntarily to her parents. From this point on counseling focussed on Sandra's use of alcohol; she admitted to hiding liquor in her room, where she would get high and sleep off the effects. Her mother frequently grounded her for rude remarks and failure to be neat or do housekeeping duties, so Sandra had plenty of opportunity to retire quietly to her room and drink. Her father took her to Alateen while he attended AA meetings, where she was able to observe his tendency to make over-close connections with younger women. At length Sandra was persuaded to enter a rehabilitation program. Here for the first time she acknowledged her prior use of many drugs, and she also revealed a history of incest with her father from the age of five. When an investigation was made, she recanted the information. Cathy was at first very angry at the referral of her daughter to a rehabilitation program, but her attitude changed when she learned of the extent of Sandra's addictive behavior. Cathy reacted with more feeling to the discovery that her daughter might be alcohol and drug dependent than to the confession of incest by Sandra or to Sandra's running away. Cathy subsequently decided the problems in her marriage could not be tolerated and moved out, leaving Sandra in Fred's custody; he then terminated Sandra's therapy.

This case raises issues of differentiation versus discipline, empowerment versus enabling, and custody/confidentiality questions. At an age when Sandra would normally be differentiating her personality in a search for her own identity, her parents pasted their marriage together by forming a team to bear down on her and isolate her in the family and community by extensive grounding. Gabarino and Gabarino (1987) suggest that overcontrol can be as damaging as undercontrol on the part of parents who may become desperate as their child becomes uncontrollable, leading to abuse. In this sense, Sandra's mother contributed to her abuse, by expecting too much of her and then abandoning her to her father, the primary abuser.

The issue of confidentiality is a difficult one with 13 to 17 year-old adolescents who are chary of their trust. In this case Sandra ran away before trust had been established with her counselor, who, of course, reported her previous overdose with pills to her parents. When work began on Sandra's substance abuse, the counselor kept confidentiality, in order to induce her to enter rehabilitation. The mother's anger had to be withstood and understood in the context of her own ambivalence about her marriage and about her commitment to the family. Although her anger soon turned to gratitude, the marriage dissolved when it no longer had the uniting focus of an uncontrollable adolescent.

Sandra's depression must also be considered as connected to her substance abuse. Her situation contained several factors associated with adolescent chemical abuse: a chemically dependent parent, absence of a parent, a shaky ego adjustment due to incest, unexpressed anger at the family situation and her parents' overcontrol, and, possibly, peer pressure; any of these may have moved her toward experimentation with chemicals which afford a brief escape from depression and anxious thoughts (Stein & Davis, 1982).

In summary, the special treatment issues in cases of abused adolescents involve the difficulty of joining with a damaged and mistrustful person who is enmeshed in a rigid system where denial and secrecy are the norm.

Motivation to change is often lacking in the adolescent when the parent makes the appointment, and another difficulty is eliciting expression of emotion from a child whose parents felt threatened by any expression of feeling (Bepko & Krestan, 1985). Art therapy may be indicated, both for the child and the family, as an avenue toward communication (see, for example, Landgarten, 1987); interpersonal communication is known to be sparse in child-abusing families (Silber, 1990). The overriding concern in most cases is for emotional relief; adolescents in one study made a point of telling their social worker that the physical injury did not bother them as much as the emotional trauma (Libbey & Bybee, 1979).

PREVENTION OF ABUSE

A wide range of preventive efforts are currently under way across the country. Some states have income tax forms with a check off box to donate a dollar to this cause. Educational programs have sprung up for parents and children, in order to intercede before rising tensions recreate old patterns of violence. Two approaches will be described here, because of their innovative character.

The Behavior Management-Artplay Program, currently sponsored by the New Jersey Children's Trust Fund serves families who are considered at risk for child abuse by reason of domestic violence or substance abuse in their backgrounds. These families are given 16 sessions of free treatment: eight family therapy sessions for individual families, and eight "artplay" sessions in which parent/child relationships are strengthened through mutual participation in quiet, nonverbal, art-type tasks, followed by support groups. After 16 sessions families are not dropped, but are referred for further therapy and/or group participation.

The rationale for use of art therapy to reduce tensions between parents and children is based on the psychological value of free self expression and acceptance of that expression (Landgarten, 1987). Art therapy is an established technique which serves to elicit self expression, build self-esteem, enable the growth of personal creativity, and reach to depths of feeling which often cannot be expressed in words. Artplay tasks are directed toward specific goals: a boundary exercise to see how a parent sets a limit and whether the child respects it; defining structure by working together constructively within certain limits; observation of the child by the parent in order to monitor their interaction, together and with others. There are exercises to elicit safe recollection of fear and anger, and others to promote a feeling of support and self-esteem.

The 55 families serviced in two years have shown a reduction in problem behaviors; their self-report questionnaires (taken every eight sessions if they continue in the program) reveal satisfaction with their growth in parent-child acceptance and the positive emotional development of the child. They tend to make use of behavior management tools, such as time-out or contracting, after they have experienced a reduction in frustration over parenting issues.

The second program provides comprehensive school-based treatment for children and was reported by Kevin Stark, Cathy Simmons Brookman, and Randy Frazier (1990) at the University of Texas. This program identifies children and adolescents who show depression on self-report measures and in interviews and offers them and their parents training designed to alleviate stress. The four basic components are (1) cognitive restructuring, attributional retraining, and covert modeling; (2) training in self-control skills (self-monitoring, self-reinforcement, and self-evaluation); (3) behavioral procedures (activity planning, assertiveness training, social skills training, relaxation, and imagery); and (4) parent training.

Because this intervention program is designed for the school setting, (meeting twice a week in small groups), and since it involves parents, who are training in parenting skills, it solves the problem of the adolescent unmotivated to seek help and the problem of the home-school gap. Although it is not primarily designed as an abuse-prevention project, this program meets the needs of high-tension families whose children are showing symptoms of the stress that can lead to abuse. Youths are said to return to a regressive state when threatened (Morgan, 1977). It is possible that in teaching these children to evaluate and assert themselves, while their parents learn skills that complement their children's training, this program intervenes at a crucial point to avert an escalating possibility of abuse.

As more and more schools achieve the establishment of mandated drug abuse programs for adolescents (cf., Alliance for change: A plan for community action on adolescent drug abuse, by J. F. Crowley, 1984), the chances increase that ongoing abuse will be identified, and potential abuse avoided.

CONCLUSION

Abuse of adolescents constitutes about one quarter of reported cases and is strongly linked to substance abuse, though no statistics have been reported. Pertinent factors in abuse of adolescents include the problems of parenting at this stage of development and the emotional trauma leading to depression that can result, whether the abuse was long or short-term. A consideration of treatment issues differentiates the problems of primary, secondary and tertiary care; four cases illustrate the family pathology involved when adolescents in chemically dependent families are abused and, themselves, abuse substances, or other children. Two preventive programs are described as possible interventions to avert the occurrence of abuse, by teaching the literal means of relating successfully between generations so that parents and children come to accept each other.

REFERENCES

Ackerman, R. J. (1987). *Children of alcoholics: A guide for parents, educators and therapists*. New York: Simon & Schuster.

American Bar Association Policy Recommendation on Youth Alcohol and Drug Problems. (1986). Washington, D.C.

Barnard, C. P. (1984). Alcoholism & incest in the family — Part I: Similar traits, common dynamics, Part II: Issues in treatment. In *Alcoholism: A family matter*, Pompano Beach, Florida: Health Communications, Inc.

Bavolek, S. J. & Henderson, H. L. (1990). Child maltreatment and alcohol abuse: Comparisons and perspectives for treatment. In R. T. Potter-Efron, & P. S. Potter-Efron, (Eds.). *Aggression, family violence and chemical dependency*. New York: The Haworth Press, Inc.

Bepko, C. & Krestan, J. A. (1985). *The responsibility trap*. New York: The Free Press.

Black, C. (1982). *It will never happen to me*. Denver, M.A.C.

Bradshaw, J. (1988). *Healing the shame that binds you*. Deerfield Beach, Florida: Health Communications, Inc.

Buckley, T. J., McCarthy, J. J., Norman, E., & Quaranta, M. A. (Eds.). (1977). *New directions in family therapy*. Oceanside, New York: Dabor Science Publications.

Caviola, A. A. (1989). Adolescent chemical dependency: Assessment & intervention issues. *New Jersey Psychologist, 39*, 8-10.

Cavaiola, A. & Schiff, M. (1988). Behavioral sequelae of physical and/or sexual abuse in adolescents. *Child Abuse and Neglect, 12*, 181-188.

Coombs, R. H. (Ed.). (1988). *The family context of adolescent drug use*. New York: The Haworth Press, Inc.

Crowley, J. F. (1984). *Alliance for change: A plan for community action on adolescent drug abuse*. Minneapolis: Community Intervention, Inc.

Crumbley, J (1985). Child and adolescent maltreatment: Implications for family therapy. In M. P. Mirkin & S. L. Koman (Eds.). *Handbook of adolescents and family therapy*. New York: Gardner Press, Inc.

Diagnostic and statistical manual of mental disorder. (1987). Washington D.C.: American Psychiatric Association.

Finkelhor, D., Gelles, R. J., Hotaling, G. T. & Straus, M., (Eds.). (1983). *The dark side of families: Current family violence research.* Beverly Hills, CA: Sage Publications.

Flanzer, J. P. (1990). Alcohol and family violence: Then to now—who owns the problem. In R. T. Potter-Efron & P. S. Potter-Efron (Eds.). *Aggression, family violence and chemical dependency.* New York: The Haworth Press, Inc.

Gabarino, J. & Gabarino, A. C. (1987). *Maltreatment of adolescents.* National Committee for Prevention of Child Abuse, Chicago.

Gabarino, J., Guttman, E. & Seeley, J. W. (1986). *The psychologically battered child.* San Francisco: Jossey Bass.

Glynn, T. J. & Haenlein, M. (1988). In R. H. Coomb, (Ed.). *The family context of adolescent drug use.* New York: The Haworth Press, Inc.

Holman, A. M. (1983). *Family assessment: Tools for understanding and intervention.* Beverly Hills: Sage Publications.

Landgarten, H. B. (1987). *Family art psychotherapy.* New York: Brunner/Mazel.

Libbey, P. & Bybee, R. (1979). The physical abuse of adolescents. *Journal of Social Issues, 35,* 101-126.

Miller, M. M. & Potter-Efron, R. T. (1990). Aggression and violence associated with substance abuse. In Potter-Efron, R. T. & Potter-Efron, P. S. (Eds.). *Aggression, family violence and chemical dependency.* New York: The Haworth Press, Inc.

Morgan, R. (1977). The battered adolescent: A developmental approach to identification and intervention. *Child abuse and neglect issues on innovation and implementation.* Proceedings of the Second Annual National Conference on Child Abuse and Neglect, Vol II. University of Texas at Austin.

Nakken, C. (1988). *The addictive personality: Roots, rituals and recovery.* Minneapolis: Hazeldon Educational Materials.

Potter-Efron, R. T. (1990). Differential diagnosis of physiological psychiatric and sociocultural conditions associated with aggression and substance abuse. In R. T. Potter-Efron & P. S. Potter-Efron (Eds.). *Aggression, family violence and chemical dependency.* New York: The Haworth Press, Inc.

Potter-Efron, R. T. & Potter-Efron, P. S. (1985). Family violence as a treatment issue with chemically dependent adolescents. *Alcoholism Treatment Quarterly, 2,* 1-15.

Sanford, L. T. (1982). *The silent children: A parent's guide to the prevention of child sexual abuse.* New York: McGraw-Hill.

Selekman, M. (1989). Taming chemical monsters: Cybernetic-systemic therapy with adolescent substance abusers. *Journal of Strategic and Systemic Therapies, 8,* 5-9.

Sgroi, S. M. (1982). *Handbook of clinical intervention in child abuse.* Lexington, MA: D. C. Heath and Company.

Silber, S. (1990). Conflict negotiation in child abusing and nonabusing families. *Journal of Family Psychology, 3,* 368.

Smith, K. (1990). Suicidal behavior in school aged youth. *School Psychology Review, 19,* 186-195.

Stark, K. D., Brookman, C. S., & Frazier, R. (1990). A comprehensive school-based treatment program for depressed children. *School Psychology Quarterly*, 5, 111-140.

Stein, M. D. & Davis, J. K. (1982). *Therapies for adolescents*. San Francisco: Jossey-Bass.

Trepper, T. S. & Barrett, M. J. (1989). *Systemic treatment of incest: A therapeutic handbook*. New York: Brunner/Mazel.

Adolescence, Chemical Dependency and Pathological Gambling

William L. Pursley

SUMMARY. From a review of the problem of adolescence, adolescents from dysfunctional families, the nature and extent of chemical dependency and pathological gambling among adolescents, and the definition of that experience as addiction, it is clear that there is a growing need for concern. Treatment using a cognitive behavioral, relapse prevention model seems best suited to the adolescent addictive experience because it focuses attention on the primary aspects of the disorder while helping to address the adolescent's developmental needs. The key to successful treatment is contingent upon two interrelated goals: an accurate and comprehensive family assessment must occur; an indepth cognitive/behavioral assessment must be undertaken with the addicted adolescent.

To date there has been a plethora of research regarding adolescent substance abuse and chemical dependency. It is clear that it is a growing problem that must be studied (Kaufman, 1985). However, there has been little focus on pathological gambling among adolescents. The few studies that have been done, conclude that it is a problem whose time has come (Lesieur & Klein, 1987). Akin to chemical dependency the self-reports of adult pathological gamblers describe a pattern beginning well before age 17 (Custer, 1985). From that premise, a study of normal/abnormal adolescent development, coupled with a clearer view of how excessive behavior develops into problems, should allow clinicians to become more aware of

William L. Pursley holds a doctorate (EdD) in the psychology of addiction, and is certified as Alcohol Counselor (CAC) and Compulsive Gambling Counselor (CCGC). Dr. Pursley has worked in the field of addiction since 1973; at St. Clares-Riverside Medical Center since 1975. At St. Clares-Riverside Medical Center, in Boonton Township, NJ, he is presently Director of the Alcohol/Chemical Dependency/Pathological Gambling Services. In addition, he has a private practice for addicts and their families.

© 1991 by The Haworth Press, Inc. All rights reserved.

what part adolescent risk-taking behavior plays in creating a disorder of impulse control. In addition, since human beings live in a social culture, (Berger & Luchman, 1966) could the American emphasis on external image, craving for power and control, denial and dishonesty play a role in creating the American addictive personality? As adolescents are easily influenced by the media in marketing and advertising of this personality, what changes would need to be made to stop what appears to be a trend toward adolescent addictions of all types? The issues of adolescence, dysfunctional homes, chemical dependency and pathological gambling will be addressed in the hope of providing questions and insights into the nature of the problem and the ways to combat it.

THE PROBLEM OF ADOLESCENCE

Growing up, moving beyond childhood, into adulthood, has always been hard. To survive that developmental phase, called adolescence, and emerge intact has always been, and will always remain difficult. Today, surviving adolescence has become a problem. From the many studies of the adolescent phase (Lerner & Shea, 1980; Kahn & Wright, 1980; King, 1980) it is a time of intense questioning, searching for meaning, coupled with the need to develop autonomy through developing identity. Erikson's (1972) emphasis on the stages of adolescent development provides an excellent guide into an understanding of this difficult growth period. According to Erikson, the major task of the adolescent is the establishment of a stable identity. This requires a questioning of values, a separating (rebelling) from parental figures — all leading toward autonomy. Because of adolescent insecurity, indecisiveness, inferiority and role confusion, an identity crisis develops, creating obstacles in the normal growth process. Erikson noted that the adolescent period involves a crisis in self-definition. To resolve this crisis, one must adopt an ideology (attitudes, values, beliefs) that coincides with the behavioral prescription for one's role.

Adolescent development is influenced by interactions between relationships, environments, etc. As the adolescent searches to form an identity, the process will be helped or hindered through the interactional process between family, friends, institutions and himself/herself (Lerner & Shea, 1982).

Another aspect of adolescent growth has to do with moral behavior, thought to be a core dimension of the person's adaption to his/her world. No matter how moral development and behavior are played out by the individual, it reflects the adjustment of the person to society, and would explain why some adolescents choose to obey laws and conform to social institutions, while others do not. Through family and peer influences, adolescents develop moral thoughts and behaviors which conform to parental (or group norms) or become a unique dimension of their personal identity. As they grow toward an integration of thoughts and behaviors they resolve the crisis and gain comfort with their role definition (Kohlberg, 1979).

During adolescence, there is the need for acceptance, a need for outlets of expression in physical, intellectual and emotional fields, and a need for standards with which to conform or to rebel. There is a special need to be treated as a unique individual — with the same respect that adults automatically give to one another. There is the need to be independent. It comes as no surprise, therefore, that adolescents model adult behaviors at an early age — they smoke, drink and gamble to express their growth toward maturity.

To further explain the developmental process of adolescence, Anna Freud (1958) defines the issues of adolescence as the task of dealing with impulses. Using her outline as a guide might explain why adolescents are vulnerable to adjustment, impulse control, behavioral, and psychoactive substance abuse disorders. The task of dealing with impulses is difficult at best when an adolescent must also define right and wrong and behave in accordance with that belief. Moving toward autonomy while establishing intimacy outside of parents forces adolescents to struggle with issues of love for self while defining who they are. Having come to see themselves as dependent children wanting to be adults, adolescents revolt against that which stands in their way. Learning to give as well as receive while gaining pleasure in mastery, demands that adolescents venture outside of themselves, become involved in healthy activities and grow toward a balance between too much or too little involvement with self or others.

ADOLESCENTS
FROM DYSFUNCTIONAL HOMES

Having established the obstacles in normal, healthy adolescent development, attention will be directed to the dynamics of a dysfunctional home. David Gelman (1990) states ". . . as a generation, today's teenagers face more adult strength stresses than their predecessors did — at a time when adults are much less available to help them." It is ironic that at a time when experts see how much adolescents depend on adults for healthy development, the divorce rate is 50 percent. From 40 to 50 percent of teenagers live in single parent homes headed by working mothers, thereby placing teenagers more on their own than ever (Gelman, 1990). Adoles-

cents have more access than ever to fast cars, fast drugs, easy sex, as well
as other options that can have devastating results. In today's world the
only things uniting adolescents are the things they can plug into. Rich or
poor, they have their "Walkmans," VCR's, TVs, and personal tele-
phones further isolating them from society. With that backdrop of the
'90s, it is clear why it has become increasingly more difficult to experience a healthy adolescence.

To see why psychoactive substance abuse, especially alcohol dependence, and pathological gambling present major problems for adolescents,
requires looking into the homes that create dysfunction. There seems to be
a very clear correlation between parents who drink/drug/gamble and their
children adopting the same behavior. Whether there is a genetic, biological link in the causal chain or an environmental influence is unclear. However, it is now apparent that from dysfunctional homes come dysfunctional adolescents. According to Harritz and Christensen (1987), the
following statistics emphasize the problem: Of the 28.6 million children
of alcoholics in the U.S. today about one third are under the age of 18.
These children have a four times greater risk of becoming alcoholic. Statistics indicate that 30 percent of fourth graders experience pressure to try
alcohol, while 33.4 percent of the nation's sixth graders have tried beer or
wine. Drug related juvenile arrests have more than tripled in certain major
cities (Detroit, New York) during the 1980s, while in Los Angeles they
have climbed from 41 arrests in 1980 to a staggering 1,719 in 1987. The
number of crack users in the Northeast is said to be increasing at a rate of
2,000 per day. Twenty-five percent of children in the fourth grade say
they feel pressure to use drugs while 11 percent of sixth graders begin to
use drugs while they are in that grade. Burk (1972) describes the problem:

> The children of alcoholics are vulnerable. They are vulnerable to the
> effects of poor or inadequate models who are alcoholics and who
> happen to be their parents. They are exposed to complex patterns of
> behavior that show adults coping with stress by the use of alcohol,
> and they are exposed to mass media that encourages alcohol use as a
> necessary accompaniment of human pleasure and socialization.
> When the child is younger, excessive alcohol use may appear as an
> effective social stimulant and an anxiety reduction substance, and
> thus set the stage for the latter elicitation of similar behaviors by the
> grown child. By the time the social or physical decay of chronic
> alcoholism is apparent, the child may be so reinforced and patterned
> toward excessive alcohol use that the outcome is certain. If thought

of in this way, it is surprising that all the children of alcoholics do not become alcoholics themselves. (p. 191)

A study done in California (Jacobs, Marston, Singer, Wedaman, Little & Veizades, 1989) with 844 randomly selected ninth-to-twelfth-grade students reported that without exception, children of parents described as problem gamblers showed higher levels of use of alcohol, cocaine, amphetamines, increased overeating, and gambling. Most striking was the finding that 75 percent of those whose parents were problem gamblers reported an age of onset for gambling before 11 years of age. These subjects consistently rated themselves as much more insecure than their peers; feeling a greater need for success; more often reported "poor mental state"; and felt emotionally "down" and "unhappy with life and myself."

In addition to the abuse of children from parental alcohol, drug and gambling dependence, there is also physical and sexual abuse. However, according to Garbarino (1987), family dysfunction mainly is the result of psychological/emotional abuse that takes five forms.

1. Rejecting: The parent refuses to acknowledge the child's worth and the legitimacy of the child's needs.
2. Isolating: The child is removed from important social experiences leading the child to experience himself as alone.
3. Ignoring: The adult is physically present, but is absent emotionally and psychologically.
4. Terrorizing: The parent assaults a child with words — instilling fear, and frightens the child, leading the child to experience the world as hostile.
5. Corrupting: The adult "mis-socializes" the child, or overstimulates the child, or leads the child to engage in destructive behavior, and reaffirms the child's deviance.

Growing up in a dysfunctional home where there is emotional and psychological maltreatment, children experience inconsistencies between the overly generous to the overly harsh parenting style. The parent's failures, frustrations and needs are projected as if the children are to blame. By adolescence, many have already suffered so much confusion that the developmental process leads to a distortion in self-identification. When children are told repeatedly that they are "no good," that they are "lazy and ugly," it is very difficult for them to believe otherwise.

Whitfield, (1987) Beattie, (1987) and Wegscheider-Cruse, (1985) have pointed out that in addition to the parent who is an addict, there may also be the parent who is codependent. Together, the addict plus the codependent equals a codependent or addicted adolescent whom Beattie, (1987) defines thus:

> A codependent person is one who has let another person's behavior affect him or her, and who is obsessed with controlling that person's behavior. In a home where this is occurring, it is very hard for an adolescent to grow and develop a normal identity and a sense of individuality, while moving toward independence.

John Bradshaw, (1988) explains what happens to a child growing up in this family system:

> When a child is born to these shame-based parents, the deck is stacked from the beginning. The job of parents is to model. Modeling includes how to be a man or woman; how to relate intimately to another person; how to acknowledge and express emotions; how to fight fairly; how to have physical, emotional and intellectual boundaries; how to communicate; how to cope and survive life's unending problems; how to be self-disciplined, how to love oneself and another. Shame-based parents cannot do any of these. They simply don't know how . . . Needy, shame-based parents cannot possibly take care of their children's needs. The child is shamed whenever he or she is needy because the child's needs clash with the parent's needs. The child grows up and becomes an adult. But underneath the mask of adult behavior there is a child who was neglected. This needy child is insatiable. What that means is that when the child becomes an adult, there is a "hole in his soul." He can never get enough as an adult. Adults make what they get be enough and work harder to get more the next time. An adult child can't get enough because it's really a child's needs that are in question.

When adolescents grow up in a materialistic, dishonest culture that emphasizes excessiveness, externals and the easy life, hopes for their successful integration fade. With the pervasiveness of addiction, family dysfunction and codependency, it is no surprise that more and more adolescents are being treated for various psychological/behavioral problems while suicides continue to increase. Given the trauma experienced in childhood, coupled with the poor impulse control of early adolescence and the modeling of adult behaviors, it is to be expected that adolescents would be vulnerable to alcohol/drug dependencies and pathological gambling.

ADOLESCENT CHEMICAL DEPENDENCY
AND PATHOLOGICAL GAMBLING

It is difficult to explain the etiology of chemical dependency and pathological gambling among adolescents, other than what has been described thus far. It is widespread and increasing among those who are the most vulnerable. According to Gelman, (1990) contributory factors may be that youngsters between the ages of 12 and 17 watch TV an average of twenty-two hours a week, or about three hours a day. As only 34.9 percent of Hispanic teenagers and 39.2 percent of Black teenagers can read proficiently by age 13, a tendency on their part to quit school has increased. Since adolescents are deeply influenced by the mass media, watching TV not only increases the desire for the "good life," it also strengthens the potential that they will drop out of high school. The time spent viewing TV guarantees that many adolescents will not develop or cultivate basic reading and writing skills — skills that are mandatory if people expect to graduate from high school.

The temptation to escape the pain of failure increases the vulnerability of adolescents toward a pathological dependency. Data from the New Jersey Casino Control Commission (June, 1989) monitoring adolescents at casinos in Atlantic City shows a marked increase every year among the adolescents prevented from entering (over 200,000 in 1988) and those escorted from the casino (over 40,000 in 1988). In addition, the New Jersey Council on Compulsive gambling hot line (June, 1990) reports that calls from 13-19 year-olds have increased every year and now average seven percent of all calls received. When one realizes the abundance of lottery tickets and drugs available in the inner cities of New Jersey and that many adults are modeling behaviors which include their purchase and use — the message is clear. Teenagers from the inner city may see their ticket out as either "a dollar and a dream" or selling drugs. It is questionable, therefore, whether clinicians are not seeing the tip of the iceberg with regard to the problem of pathological gambling in adolescence.

Adolescents are living in an addictive environment. From addictive homes, to the drug and gambling infected streets, schools and playgrounds, adolescents are bombarded with the temptation to get high. From pushers and pimps who model success, to TV and the mass media that preaches externals (the right clothes, shoes, cars, etc.) to the avenue of sports and music where their idols are rich, famous and successful, they get a message of what they must do to be successful. With crack houses, bars, lottery tickets sold everywhere, and pinball, billiards and video arcades offering an easy entry into the world of drugs and gambling, how can anyone expect the most vulnerable to resist temptation? If, realizing, at the same time that the most lucrative jobs for adolescents include running numbers and delivering drugs (paying hundreds of dollars a day) can society offer an alternative powerful enough to keep adolescents from moving toward the addictive alternative? Clearly, as more and more adolescents move toward chemical dependency and pathological gambling, helpers must learn how to define, assess and treat the problem.

DEFINITIONS OF CHEMICAL DEPENDENCY AND PATHOLOGICAL GAMBLING

However chemical dependency and pathological gambling are defined, the problem is one of using diagnostic criteria that fit the adolescent population. Since it is beyond the scope of this article to argue the point and for the sake of brevity, both chemical dependency and pathological gambling are viewed as "addictions." Psychological research seeks commonalities across behaviors, as well as addictive behaviors. The definition set forth by Donovan (1988) will be utilized:

> An addiction is seen as a complex, progressive behavior pattern having biological, psychological, sociological and behavioral components. What sets this behavior pattern apart from others is the individual's overwhelmingly pathological involvement in or attachment to it, subjective compulsion to continue it, and reduced ability to exert personal control over it . . . There appears to be a dependence upon the behavior or experience, either on a physiological or a psychological level, that may lead to withdrawal distress when the individual is prevented from engaging in the behavior . . . Finally, the power of the addictive experience promotes a tendency for rapid reinstatement of the behavior pattern following a period of noninvolvement in it.

The use of this biopsychosocial model (including mental, emotional, spiritual, behavioral and social components) will help to define the addictive phenomenon in a way that integrates the broad spectrum of addicts' self-reports, while helping to guide clinicians in a treatment strategy which includes an assessment of all the psychological factors that reinforce the behavioral problems (Beck, 1977). Researchers studying pathological gambling are starting to see the efficacy of using the terms addiction and dependency (Orford & McCartney, 1990; Walker, 1989; Shaffer & Gambino, 1989). According to Orford, in spite of the differences between substance and non-substance addictions, the parallels between excessive gambling and excessive drinking are many and close.

From clinical work with chemically dependent and pathological gambling adolescents, it has been observed that there are more similarities than differences. In spite of the obvious differences between adolescents who take substances expecting results and those who place a bet expecting results, there is a commonality to the experience. Both groups of adolescent addicts expect a mood change, and escape, a relief and a way to cope with a reality that is alienating. Both want to avoid pain and increase pleasure, and both are willing to pay a high price to achieve the desired effect. Problems in living, relating, working, recreating, coping, along with financial and legal difficulties do not deter either group from stopping the behavior. To get high, to transcend the tedium of day-to-day boredom, to avoid responsibility, these adolescent addicts will risk much.

Both groups, the chemical dependency and pathological gambling adolescents, are involved in a process of repeating a behavioral pattern until it becomes ingrained—a way of life that becomes addictively enslaving. That is to say, they become products of addictive thinking, feeling, believing and behaving that has them depending upon their "fix" to elevate their mood and help them cope. Over time, the relief is reduced while the pain of not having the relief, coupled with the problems that the behavior promotes, continues to worsen. This vicious cycle reinforces the dependency, the need for relief outside of self, and the reinstatement of the behavior that the adolescent hopes will provide it. Therefore the process of addiction can be viewed in the following way:

1. Addiction as an experience, a fix-it behavior includes: mental obsession with getting high (transcending, escaping); emotional dependency upon getting high; spiritual commitment to getting high.
2. Addiction includes whatever actions, risks and prices an adolescent must pay to get high, including: losing relationships, losing jobs, losing self, losing freedom, losing meaning, purpose, direction; losing faith, trust, honesty.
3. Addiction promises escape and produces enslavement to: broken promises, shattered dreams, familial/financial/personal collapse.
4. Addiction as it promotes pain, through withdrawal and problems, reinforces the need/desire to get high (Pursley, 1984).

As this process repeats itself, as it worsens, it brings with it a greater need for relief, an inability to see oneself outside of the addiction and a refusal to see the truth of chemical dependency and pathological gambling as the problem. In explanation, this phenomenon can be classified as a compulsion, control, continuance phenomenon (Glasser, 1984). Addiction, according to self reports, compels addicts to indulge in addictive behaviors even when they promise themselves that they will not. They also are attempting to control themselves, (thoughts, feelings, beliefs, behaviors), others, and their response to the world and its demands on them. Finally they continue the behavior in spite of all adverse consequences which tend to make them think of themselves as insane.

At its core, the addictive process becomes embedded in the addict's consciousness through habituation. Over time, adolescent addicts adopt an addictive world view including attitudes, values, beliefs, perceptions, feelings, ways of coping, interactions, style of living and self statements, and all of this manifests itself in behavior (Ellis, Mc Inerney, Di Guiseppi, & Yeager, 1988). The results are the following addictive assumptions:

1. The behavior is normal ("everyone does it, society doesn't really frown on it, it is marketed as the way to enjoy life—to be an instant millionaire, all you need is a dollar and a dream").
2. The behavior is natural ("there is nothing unnatural about drinking, drugging or gambling—people from all classes of society engage in these natural relaxation pastimes").
3. The behavior is preferred ("never trust someone who does not drink, drug, or gamble because they have not tasted the fruits of life and they are so uptight they do not know the joy of playing the game") (Pursley, 1984).

As this reciprocal process progresses, the more the adolescent addict engages in it, the more normal, natural and preferred he/she believes it to be. The more normal, natural and preferred he/she believes it to be, the more he/she engages in the behavior. At some point it will seem that the adolescent addict "lives to do the behavior and does the behavior to live" (Pursley, 1984).

Both adolescence and addictions are developmental processes and can reinforce each other. When the adolescent has a need to be met, the addiction comes to the rescue to provide the solution. At the beginning of its development in adolescence, addiction provides answers to questions, anesthesia for awkwardness, people to experience it with, an identity, a place to be, something to do, an antidote for affective difficulties and an easy way to change mood. The pleasure reinforces the urge to experience the addiction making it almost impossible to see that pain and difficulty will occur. For the adolescent who has little impulse control, addiction provides instant gratification (Pursley, 1984).

According to Golden and Schwartz (1987), in early adolescence, when emotional tolerance is essential as preparation for the next phase of development, addiction anesthetizes the feeling process. As addiction gives the appearance of helping adolescents control their emotions, it will, in fact, increase mood swings while it intensifies moods.

In middle adolescence when adolescents need to organize their value system, even when it may differ from their family's addiction brings more conflicts and confusion, rather then clarity. Through addiction, cognitive impairment creates a situation in which they behave in opposition to their belief system. As they move away from their developing value system, addiction increases inadequacy while promoting the loss of self-esteem.

In late adolescence, when independence would promote individuality, addiction increases dependency upon family, the peer group and the addictive behavior itself. At a time when relationships should be less superficial, getting high, drinking and placing a bet becomes the relationship. Listening to adolescents describe their addiction in treatment, it becomes apparent how deeply "in love" and committed to the addictive relationship they really are. The deepest needs for acceptance and love become enveloped into the addictive process and replace the normal developmental process making it virtually impossible to grow into a full functioning autonomous adult. Without treatment at this stage, the identity and developmental crisis cycle will continue to plague the adolescent well into the "age of adulthood."

The effect of addiction to alcohol, drugs, and or/gambling on the adolescent's development can be summarized as follows: First, adolescents need to develop an identity which is unique to them. Searching through the behaviors available and then becoming addicted means that the search is ended. Once addicted, he or she has become a "drinker," a "drugger" or a "gambler." As such, he/she is a "top gun," a big shot, an o.k. person who is no longer plagued by the "who am I" question.

Secondly, the adolescent needs a place to be in the world and an outlet for physical expression. As an addict, he/she has defined his/her place in the world among fellow addicts and he/she has the need for physical expression met. Expression merely requires that he/she hang out with addicts, take a drink, smoke some crack or place a bet. Instead of the many, many options that exist for adolescents today, the addict simplifies the process by reducing the choice to the smallest common denominator — getting high.

Thirdly, the adolescent needs to separate, revolting against dependency by becoming independent. Since most parents, addicted or not, do not want their children to be addicted, addiction provides the adolescent with a wonderful vehicle to express rebellion against all authority and to establish a form of independence.

Fourthly, the adolescent needs to develop a system of attitudes, values and beliefs—a standard and code of ethics. Addiction gives adolescents something to believe in. When in doubt, the adolescent addict simply takes another hit, takes another drink, or places another bet and existential terror is anesthetized. Through habitual behavior, which quickly becomes an automatic response, there is no longer need to spend much time searching for the reason to live.

The fifth item is that the adolescent needs to find acceptance, love and intimacy. When close relations with friends and the opposite sex seem difficult or unrewarding, the addictive experience rescues from the loneliness and isolation. As an old saying adequately describes it, "what greater love is there in the world than the love of one drunken bum for another." As seductions, all addictions are love affairs until they deepen into the demands of "till death do us part." In that way, the intimacy need is satisfied.

Finally, the adolescent needs to be a "grown-up" individual. In the difficult and demanding world of addiction, addicts are respected for the risks they take, the crimes they commit, the arrests/imprisonments they endure and the tough exterior that makes them appear grown-up. Even if there is no respect from family or adults, it will not matter. As long as respect comes from other addicts and the "adult behavior" is praised, the need is met.

In conclusion, it is clear that addiction, be it chemical dependency or pathological gambling, has many negative consequences. For the adolescent it creates mental distortion, cognitive confusion, impaired judgement, spiritual depravity, uncontrollable mood swings, behavioral problems and an inability to grow, develop and mature into a healthy adult. It takes a normal developmental process and stops it from following its natural course. It takes a child of promise and promotes pain through the process of reliance on externals (the drug, the bet) robbing the child of internalized integrity.

TREATMENT OF CHEMICAL DEPENDENCY/ PATHOLOGICAL GAMBLING IN ADOLESCENTS

Turning attention to the treatment of adolescent chemically dependent and/or pathological gambling addicts, it is apparent that this stage of intervention is as complicated as the addictions themselves. Just as it is difficult to get adults into treatment, so it is with adolescents. In addictions treatment, until behavior creates the necessity for educational, legal, medical or parental intervention, addicts continue their addictive involvement. Even when confronted with factual evidence, addicts continue to discount it through rationalizing while making promises to do better. Typically pressure is required from many sources to get the adolescent to "agree" to treatment. Since the formal strategy for interventions is readily available (Johnson, 1973) there is no need to discuss it here. However, one major difference in the treatment of adolescents is that family therapy is, at times, necessary to maintain the adolescent in treatment. Often it is the parents who call for help with their uncontrollable children. In addition to an "intervention," family therapy can be used as a means to engage the adolescent in treatment with the family and hopefully, at some point, in individual and group therapy as well (Fishman, Stanton & Rosman, 1982).

David Treadway (1989) has found some success with adolescents who would otherwise resist or refuse treatment altogether. He writes, ". . . the hardest part of working with adolescents is that, when it comes to a confrontation over control, many kids are willing to die in order to win." Thus, Treadway suggests six steps:

1. *Engage the whole system:* (School and counselor, probation officer, department of social services workers, clergyman, etc.)

2. *Assessment:* The question of whether the acting out behavioral problems in school and home is primary or if addiction is primary must be assessed and clarified. Therapists must be careful to work with the denial structure of the parents as well as the adolescent to determine if chemical dependency or pathological gambling is the problem.

3. *Empower the parents:* Therapists must help parents to devise a therapeutic agenda that will help to engage the child in treatment and will help to set behavioral limits at home. By engaging the children in creating the rules and consequences it becomes possible for the parents to have control while gaining adolescent compliance. Through negotiation and enforcement parents can become a part of the solution by allowing the adolescents to become responsible for their behavior along with its consequences.

4. *The crisis of change:* Once the parents are empowered and the rules and consequences have been established, it is normal for the adolescent to question and challenge the change to see if the parents are serious and committed. If the diagnosis is one of primary chemical dependency or pathological gambling it may be that the adolescent will be unable to comply, leading to the need for primary chemical dependency/pathological gambling treatment. It is, at this point, that an intervention regarding

chemical dependency/pathological gambling can lead to an inpatient treatment setting or an intensive outpatient program for the adolescent.

5. *Restraint from change:* Once the crisis has been completed and the adolescent is now functioning better, the therapy becomes awkward because the family does not know what to address next. At this stage the therapist must help the family to stay focused on the issues of early recovery and helping the adolescent to maintain behavioral change. If at this stage a relapse occurs, the family learns to deal with it successfully, helping the adolescent to regain recovery.

6. *Individuation:* Once the members of the family are feeling more independent and competent, it is time to deal with specific issues. It is the goal of therapy during this last stage to enable the family members to individuate and facilitate the adolescent's autonomy and independence. Since disengagement is very difficult this stage may take some time to complete (Treadway, 1989, pp. 140-158).

Unlike the clarity that can result rapidly in adult assessments, the "chicken or egg" phenomenon related to adolescents is difficult to resolve. Is this an adolescent developmental issue or chemical dependency or pathological gambling or an oppositional or conduct disorder, or a combination that needs to be treated? Roger Meyer (1986) describes the possible types of relationships between psychopathology and addictive disorders. He lists them as psychopathology as a risk factor, psychopathology as a modifier of the course of the addictive disorder, psychiatric symptoms of chronic intoxications, and psychiatric disorders as a consequence in use.

Treatment professionals must learn to deal with adolescents, taking all determinants into account. Given the tendency of adolescents (who view themselves as immortal and without problems) to deny difficulties or to view them as caused by adult perceptions, assessment is difficult. Collecting as much information as possible from as many collateral sources as possible helps to break through the adolescents' tendency to rationalize their addictive problems (Fischer, 1978).

The assessment should include the adolescent, the parents and siblings, the school teachers/counselors, the parole officer and the social service worker. From each of the sources, the assessment should ascertain a history of drinking, drugging and gambling, medical history, a history of school performance, a history of any type of legal or financial difficulties, and specifically any and all types of behavioral problems. Included must be a history of any attempts to engage in therapy or attain mental health, chemical dependency or pathological gambling treatment for the adolescent or family.

Since the assessment phase of treatment is crucial to a successful outcome, it becomes very important for therapists to have a clinical understanding of all the masks that chemical dependency and pathological gambling can wear. In addition to the fact that most adolescent CD's and PG's can also be diagnosed as conduct, identity and adjustment disordered, it is essential to determine which is primary.

Alcohol/drug use among children has stayed constant during the last two decades, increasing during the course of adolescence, producing a significant number of diagnosable chemically dependent (Christiansen & Goldman, 1983; Downs & Robertson, 1982; Huba & Bentler, 1980). Based on the total numbers of users, coupled with the increases in highway fatalities, it can be projected that as many as five percent of the adolescent population suffer from chemical dependency.

Since research into pathological gamblers generally is limited in both number and quality, it is hard to place an accurate figure on the number of PG adolescents. However, from a landmark study in New Jersey (Lesieur & Klein, 1987) among 892 high school juniors and seniors, many conclusions can be drawn. Twenty-two percent gambled at least once a week, despite parental objection; 15 percent admitted lying about their wagering games; 10 percent used illegal means to finance their gambling; six percent were unable to repay their gambling debts; and 5.7 percent were considered to be pathological gamblers. These numbers parallel the adult PG's.

The assessment process should include the extent of the individuals' drinking and/or drug taking. Accurate results can be obtained by using the M.A.S.T. or the twenty questions from Alcoholics/Narcotics Anonymous. To assess the extent of the gambling, the South Oaks Gambling Screen (SOGS) or the twenty questions from Gamblers Anonymous can be used. Even though geared for adults they can provide a valuable resource tool for assessment.

In addition to a detailed behavioral assessment, it is crucial to have a detailed cognitive addictions assessment as well. The results of research (Smith, Canter & Robin, 1989) indicate that just like adults, adolescents develop a set of expectations about alcohol and drugs from various sources. These expectancies seem to be reciprocally determined and developed through observational learning. Two very strong sources of direct influence are parents/family interactional problems leading to a reduction in social coping skills and the adolescent peer group's approval of addiction. Evidence (Donovan & Marlatt, 1980) suggests that specific expectancies for alcohol exist in young adolescents before extensive drinking experience has been acquired. It may be that the same holds true for gambling given the commonalities in the way addictions start among young people (Griffiths, 1990). It is imperative therefore, that adolescent perceptions about drinking/drugging/gambling, family/peer relationships, as well as their view of themselves in the world, be completely assessed. If denial persists, the assessment of the historical, behavioral and cognitive addictive components can be used to gain treatment compliance.

Once the adolescent is engaged in treatment, using a cognitive behavioral model of relapse prevention, adolescents can be taught how to recover from addiction. Just as it is true with the adult addictive population, once the diagnosis of chemical dependency or pathological gambling is established, treatment must focus attention upon and address the addiction specifically. Research (Kendall & Braswell, 1985) shows that the cognitive behavioral model of treatment not only works with impulsive children but also with chronically dependent and pathological gambling adolescents as well (Ellis, McInerney, DiGuiseppi & Yeager, 1988). It is primarily a psycho-educational, behavioral-change relapse-prevention approach to a disorder that interferes with an adolescent's perceptions, values, attitudes, beliefs, interactions, feelings and behaviors. Since this approach fits the adolescent experience as well as blending with a twelve step (Alcoholics Anonymous, Gamblers Anonymous) model of self-help, it is the treatment of choice to promote recovery. By specifically addressing the mental, emotional, spiritual, behavioral and social aspects of addiction, adolescents can focus on a change strategy that creates self-mastery. Through a process of facing the addiction, making a commitment to abstinence and through learning alternative coping strategies, social skills, resistance to temptation to drink, drug or gamble again, the adolescent becomes empowered to make a choice between relapse or recovery (Marlatt & Gordon, 1985).

The cognitive behavioral therapy approach is specifically directed toward four aspects of the addictive use of substances or addictive behaviors:

1. The relief of affective symptoms which may be contributing to or exaggerating the addiction. These symptoms include depression, anger, fear, anxiety and defeatism. Following Beck's (1976) model, chemically dependent and pathological gamblers suffer from a cognitive-based affective disorder stemming from the beliefs that "life sucks" (negativity = depression), "life is unfair" (anger = hostility), "life is threatening" (fear = anxiety, paranoia), "life owes me" (wishfulness = disappointment). Therapy must address the distorted negative self image moving

adolescent addicts to a better self concept, and an identity which allows for behavioral failure (instead of failure = "I'm no good," failure = "I can succeed if I learn from my mistakes"). Therapy must address the adolescent addict's tendency to be angry with himself/herself, as well as his or her primarily negative interpersonal-relationships. Self understanding leads to the insight that blaming is self-defeating and nonproductive. By teaching the addict to be task-oriented, he/she can challenge the anger and overpower it. Coupled with learning positive self talk ("I can deal with this," "I don't have to overreact,") he/she can learn to cool down and get through the vulnerable moment without a relapse. Therapy must address the adolescent addict's fear and anxiety that results from the threats, perceived and real, which can undermine his or her efforts in abstinence ("I'm too uptight to stay recovering," "I need some relief"). Finally, therapy must help the adolescent addict address his or her wishfulness and fantasy consciousness. Through reality therapy (Glasser, 1965), addicts can learn to focus away from the easy success and move toward achievement strategies with built in success stages based on hard work.

2. Teaching the patient to control himself or herself and his or her addiction through the use of cognitive/behavioral procedures. Much of the need/urge to do addictive things is induced through self-talk. This gives the adolescent addict excuses and rationalizations for engaging in addictive behaviors. Therapy must help the adolescent addict become more conscious of, and experienced in the use of positive, abstinence-based, self-talk. In addition, since addiction is fueled, in part, through self-defeating behaviors, adolescent addicts must find ways to reinforce abstinence through productive, life affirming behaviors. By teaching the adolescent to focus on the "here and now" tasks-at-hand, he/she can learn to develop activity schedules and increase pleasurable (nonaddictive) activities. This process will help to reinforce while helping the addict gain mastery and self control (automatic thoughts and behaviors).

3. Helping the adolescent addict become re-socialized or in some cases, socialized into "normal" society. Adolescent addicts must learn that where they go, who they spend time with and what they do will determine the rate of success or failure in their recovery. What must be taught are alternative ways of living in the world while simultaneously gaining support from others who seek accomplishment of the same goals (12-Step organizations).

4. Helping the adolescent addicts to change the "silent" perceptions and beliefs of themselves and the world, especially in regard to their ad-

dictions. These primarily negative beliefs act as obstacles in maintaining recovery, examples of which include: "I'm never going to be a success"; "why try?"; "I will always need to get high"; "once a failure, always a failure"; "I don't have a problem"; "I might as well give up and die." All of these attitudes serve as potentially self-fulfilling prophecies and all of these attitudes must be changed—if recovery is to become an obtainable way of life. According to Beck and Emery, (1977) there are four categories of self-defeating thoughts/beliefs that must be altered. The first concerns capabilities of controlling addictive behavior. The second involves excuses—the person finds "reasons" as to why he or she cannot abstain from the addiction. Thirdly, addictive thoughts intrude—a staunch belief that addictive behavior must be engaged in. Lastly, a form of self-blaming begins and the addict punishes him or herself for not living up to the standards that have been set.

Through the tools of the cognitive-behavioral approach to addictions treatment, adolescent addicts can learn to develop an abstinent-based identity; a way to make positive decisions; how to cope without relapsing; how to gain self-mastery through abstinence and behavioral change; a way to defeat addictive self-talk; how to use support groups to maintain change; ways to turn addictive assumptions into positive perceptions about self, others and his or her place in the world; and a way to become empowered in dealing with the developmental difficulties of adolescence and addiction.

The cognitive-behavioral relapse-prevention model can be used in individual, group, and family therapy with equal success. Through an assessment of expectancies, perceptions and beliefs about the addictive experience, the adolescent identity, the peer relationships and the family, the adolescent can learn to focus on individual responsibility to stop placing blame, to accept the problem and to start recovery (Schlesinger, 1988). Through behavioral change contracting, adolescent addicts can learn to behave in a productive way in the home, among peers and in society. Through involvement with others who model successful abstinence (A.A., N.A., and G.A.) adolescents can learn self-mastery and self efficacy (Bandura, 1977).

Since interpersonal conflicts and peer pressure are major aspects of the adolescent and addictive developmental process, the treatment of choice is group therapy. Through the group process, adolescent addicts can learn how to abstain while developing a positive identity. They, in the group setting, gain support for successful recovery while their tendency to minimize and misdefine problems, can be confronted. During the process of

identification with peers who are recovering, adolescents can become empowered to achieve a normal behavioral pattern of abstinent-based living.
As Philip Flores (1974) writes:

> Frequently cited advantages for treating addicts in group include such factors as: peer support/peer pressure; opportunities for addicts to learn that they are not alone or unique in their personal hell; opportunities in learning about themselves by identifying with others and by interacting interpersonally with others on a meaningful and emotional level (p. 1).

Addressing the two reasons why most people seek help—isolation and demoralization, Jerome Frank (1974) argues eloquently for the use of group.

> In individual therapy, the only source of information is the therapist; in the group, other members also serve as sources of feedback, as models and as guides. In general, interactions among group members and between group members provide all members with new information, with tools to combat their demoralization, and ways to support their self-esteem. In addition, group interactions arouse members emotionally, force confrontations with their assumptive systems and their social realities and help facilitate transfer of gains into daily life (p. 276).

In the group format, adolescent addicts (through the commonality of their experience) help each other to define the high risk problem areas within the adolescent addictive process. Among these danger points are: drinking, drugging, gambling, compulsive spending, exercising, thrill-seeking, forms of escapism, dieting and overeating. At the same time they can help each other understand the need and the means to live a balanced and more comfortable addiction free adolescent way of life which includes laughter, pleasure and fun.

FUTURE DIRECTIONS

There are both growing numbers of adolescents who are seriously troubled, and little awareness among clinicians about chemical dependency and pathological gambling adolescents. Much research needs to be carried out. The following is a list of research areas that must be studied if clinicians plan to address the problem of adolescent chemical dependency and pathological gambling successfully:

 1. Degree of risk-taking as a precursor to various types of addictive behaviors.
 2. The societal emphasis on externals such as money, power, prestige, clothes, and cars, as an influence on adolescent addiction.
 3. The point at which behavior becomes compulsive/addictive.
 4. Whether or not the competitive society breeds compulsive behavior.
 5. The use of cognitive/behavioral relapse-prevention model of treatment with pathological gamblers.
 6. The problem of video arcades, pinball and billiards, the adolescent version of casinos.
 7. Adolescent assessment tools for chemical dependency and pathological gambling.
 8. Longitudinal studies of the effects of CD and PG parents on children must take place.
 9. More comprehensive study of adolescent gambling practices.
 10. The relationship between drinking/drugging/gambling among adolescents and its impact on adult addiction.

CONCLUSION

The issue of adolescence, chemical dependency and pathological gambling deserves a continual focus from research. As our society continues to emphasize the externals of power, money and fame, at the expense of promoting integrity and independence, clinicians will continue to see many troubled teenagers. Many of these will be suffering from conduct, adjustment and identity disorders. Others will be suffering from chemical dependency or pathological gambling. Some will be suffering from a combination of disorders.

Because of the importance of the developmental process of growth toward maturity, adolescents deserve the best that treatment professionals can give them. To be able to provide the best, clinicians must continue to study the needs of adolescents and the relationship between specific needs and the tendency toward addictive behaviors. At the same time, clinicians need to study what part society plays in creating an environment that moves adolescents toward the addictive experience. Prevention and treatment efforts must take all of this into account to provide teenagers with the best chance to move toward a healthy adulthood.

To provide adolescents with the most focused treatment that can adequately fit their needs, all treatment professionals must learn as much as possible about chemical dependency and pathological gambling. These must be viewed as entities unto themselves, rather than as undiagnosed symptoms of other problems. Until this recognition occurs, many adolescents will be misdiagnosed, mistreated and misguided in their attempts to grow into adulthood.

Longitudinal studies must be started which will address the influence of drug and gambling saturated environments, and its impact upon adolescents in producing adult addicts. Specific studies need to determine if pinball, billiards and video games are the adolescent forms of adult casino gambling and if one form influences the other. If research correlates influences from the home, the social setting and the psychological cognition and behavior of adolescents with addictions, two major accomplishments will occur in the field. Firstly, an innovative treatment will be provided, that is more comprehensive in nature than are existing treatments; as such, this treatment will be capable of focusing on the specific needs of adolescents who are suffering from addictions.

REFERENCES

Bandura, A. (1977). *Social Learning Theory*. Englewood Cliffs, N.J.: Prentice Hall.

Beattie, M. (1987). *Codependent No More*. Center City, Minn.: Hazelden.

Beck, A.T. (1976). *Cognitive Therapy and Emotional Disorders*. New York: New American Library.

Beck, A.T. and Emery, G. (1977). *Cognitive Therapy of Substance Abuse*. Philadelphia, Pa.: Center for Cognitive Therapy.

Berger, P.L. and Luchman, T. (1967). *The Social Construction of Reality*. New York: Anchor Books.

Bradshaw, J. (1988). *Healing The Shame That Binds You*. Deerfield Beach, Fl.: Health Communications, Inc.

Burk, E. (1972). Some contemporary issues in child development and the children of alcoholic parents. *Annals of New York Academy of Sciences. 197*, 189-197.

Christiansen, B.A. and Goldman, M.S. (1983). Alcohol-related expectancies versus demographic/background variables in the prediction of adolescent drinking. *Journal of Consulting and Clinical Psychology. 51*, 249-257.

Custer, R. and Milt, H. (1985). *When Luck Runs Out*. New York: Facts on File Publications.

Donovan, D. (1988). Assessment of Addictive Behaviors, In D. Donovan and G.A. Marlatt (Eds). *Assessment of Addictive Behaviors*. New York: Guilford Press, *4,5*.

Donovan, D. and Marlatt, G.A. (1980). Assessment of expectancies and behaviors associated with alcohol consumption: A cognitive-behavioral approach. *Journal of Studies on Alcoholism. 43*, 1153-1185.

Downs, W.R. and Robertson, J.R. (1982). Adolescent alcohol consumption by age and sex respondent. *Journal of Studies on Alcoholism. 43*, 1027-1032.

Ellis, A., Mc Inerney, J.F., Di Guiseppi, R., & Yeager, R.J. (1988). *Rational Emotive Therapy with Alcoholics and Substance Abusers*. New York: Pergamon Press.

Eriksen, E.H. (1972). *Childhood and Society*. New York: W.W. Norton and Co., Inc.

Fischer, J. (1978). Psychotherapy of adolescent alcohol abusers. In S. Zimberg, J. Wallace, and S. Blume (Eds.). *Practical Approaches to Alcoholism Psychotherapy*. New York: Plenum Press.

Fishman, Stanton, & Rosman, (1982). Treating families of adolescent drug abusers in M. Stanton & T. Todd (Eds). *The Family Therapy of Drug Abuse and Addiction*. New York: Guilford Press.

Flores, P. (1988). *Group Psychotherapy With Addicted Populations*. New York: The Haworth Press, Inc.

Frank, J.D. (1974). *Persuasion and Healing*. New York: Schocken Books.

Freud, A. (1958). *Adolescence: Psychoanalytic Study of the Child*. New York: International University Press.

Garbarino, J. (1987). What is psychological maltreatment? In L.P. Lipsitt (Ed). *When Children Need Help*. Providence, R.I.: Manisses Communications Group.

Gelman, D. (1990). A much riskier passage. *Newsweek: The New Teens*.

Glasser, W. (1984). *Control Theory*. New York: Harper and Row.

Glasser, W. (1965). *Reality Therapy*. New York: Harper and Row.

Golden, L. and Klein, M.S. (1987). Treatment as a rehabilitation process in adolescent development and chemical dependency. *Alcoholism Treatment Quarterly. 4*, 36-38.

Griffiths, M.D. (1990). The cognitive psychology of gambling. *Journal of Gambling Studies. 6*, 31-42.

Harrity, A.S. and Christensen, A.B. (1987). *Kids, Drugs and Alcohol*. White Hall, Va.: Betterway Pub.

Huba, G.J. and Bentler, P.M. (1980). The role of peer and adult models for drug taking at different stages of adolescence. *Journal of Youth and Adolescence. 9*, 449-465.

Jacobs, D.F., Marston, A.R., Singer, R.D., Wedaman, K., Little, T. and Veizades, J. (1989). Children of problem gamblers. *Journal of Gambling Behavior. 5*, 261-268.

Johnson, V. (1973). *I'll Quit Tomorrow*. New York: Harper and Row.

Kahn, J. and Wright, S.W. (1980). *Human Growth and Development of Personality*. New York: Pergamon Press.

Kaufman, E. (1985). Adolescent substance abusers and family therapy. In M.P. Merkin, and S.L. Koman (Eds). *Handbook of Adolescents and Family Therapy*. New York: Garden Press, 245-254.

Kendall, P.C. and Braswell, L. (1985). *Cognitive Behavioral Therapy for Impulsive Children*. New York: Guilford Press.

King, S.H. (1980). Coping and growth in adolescence. In S.I. Harrison and J.F. Mc Dermott (Eds). *New Directions in Childhood Psychopathology*. New York: International University Press, Inc. *1*, 206-219.

Lerner, R.M. and Shea, J.A. (1982). Social behavior in Adolescence. In B.J. Wolman (Ed). *Handbook of Developmental Psychology*. Englewood Cliffs, N.J.: Prentice Hall, 503-525.

Lesieur, H.R. and Klein, R. (1987). Pathological gambling among high school students. *Addictive Behaviors. 12*, 129-135.

Marlatt, G.A. and Gordon, J.R. (1985). *Relapse Prevention*. New York: Guilford Press.

Meyer, R. (1986). *Psychopathology and Addictive Disorders*. New York: Guilford Press.

Orford, J. (1985). *Excessive Appetites: A Psychological View of Addictions*. New York: John Wiley and Sons.

Orford, J. and Mc Cartney, J. (1990). Is excessive gambling seen as a form of dependency? Evidence from the community and the clinic. *Journal of Gambling Studies. 6*, 139-152.

Pursley, W. (1984). *Alcohol Abusers in Treatment at St. Clare's: A Reflection Upon My Work as a Clinician Moving Toward Theoretical and Psychological Grounding*. Unpublished doctoral dissertation, Teaneck, N.J.: Fairleigh Dickinson University.

Schlesinger, S.E. (1988). Cognitive-behavioral approaches to family treatment of addictions. In N. Epstein, S. Schlesinger, and W. Dryden (Eds). *Cognitive-Behavioral Therapy with Families*. New York: Brunner/Mazel.

Shaffer, H.J. and Gambino, B. (1989). The epistemology of addictive disease: gambling as predicament. *Journal of Gambling Behavior. 5*, 211-229.

Smith, M.B., Canter, W.A., and Robin, A.L. (1989). A path analysis of an adolescent drinking behavior model derived from problem behavior theory. *Journal Studies Alcohol. 50*, 128-142.

Treadway, D. (1989). *Before It's Too Late*. New York: W.W. Norton and Co.

Walker, M.B. (1989). Some problems with the concept of gambling addiction: should theories of addiction be generalized to include excessive gambling? *Journal of Gambling Behavior. 5*, 179-200.

Wegschneider-Cruse, S. (1985). *Choice Making: For Codependents, Adult Children and Spirituality Seekers*. Pompano Beach, Fl.: Health Communications, Inc.

Whitfield, C.L. (1987). *Healing the Child Within*. Pompano Beach, Fl.: Health Communications, Inc.

Eating Disorders
and Chemical Dependency
Among Students

Victor B. Stolberg
Dianne DeValve

SUMMARY. This paper explores the relationships between eating disorders and chemical dependency factors. Various eating disorders are described. Discussion of addiction concerns recognizes the commonalities of etiology. A sample of Black students (N = 374) at a medium-sized, public, eastern community college was administered sections of the Core Instrument, Health Locus of Control Scale, Satisfaction With Life Scale, and Compulsive Eating Scale. Respective chemical dependency factors examined were for tobacco, alcohol, marijuana, and cocaine, as well as reported family history of chemical dependency. These factors were compared with measures of eating disorders, health locus of control, and satisfaction with life. No strong associations were found linking eating disorders and the chemical dependency factors examined in this study within the same individual. Although strong positive correlations were found between the age of first use and the frequency of use within the last year of the various drugs that were considered. Practical suggestions are included, along with a discussion of treatment commonalities.

INTRODUCTION

Compulsive eating and chemical dependency appear to have become increasingly prevalent during the last several decades. Food abuse can be viewed as a particular form of substance abuse, or, in other words, chemi-

---

Victor B. Stolberg, MA, MS, MSEd, MAH, EdM, CEAP is Lecturer/Counselor at Essex County College, Newark, NJ and Assistant Director of the Higher Education Consortium for Drug Abuse Prevention in Northern New Jersey. Dianne DeValve, MA, CRC, CADC, is in private practice in Union, NJ.

© 1991 by The Haworth Press, Inc. All rights reserved.

cal dependency. Chemical dependency, in general, includes alcohol abuse, alcoholism, drug abuse, and drug addiction. Compulsive eating, anorexia nervosa, and bulimia nervosa are examples of eating disorders. They are all serious problems that can have life-threatening physical as well as psychological consequences.

The phenomena of eating disorders (Bennett & Gurin, 1982; Bruch, 1973; Cauwels, 1983; Haskew & Adams, 1984; Kano, 1986) and chemical use (Cahalan, Cisin, & Crossley, 1969; Gold, 1986; Johnston, O'Malley, Bachman, 1988; Ryser, 1983; Vaillant, 1983) have been extensively studied. These behaviors, both eating disorders (e.g., Bilich, 1988-89; Dunn & Ondercin, 1981; Halmi, Falk, & Schwartz, 1981; Katzman, Wolchik, & Braver, 1984; Pyle, Halvorson, & Mitchell, 1986; Steiner-Adair, 1988-89) and chemical use (e.g., Engs, 1977; Humphrey, Stephens, & Allen, 1983; Sherry & Stolberg, 1987; Stolberg, 1989, 1990; Temple, 1987) have even been examined among college students. In a study of college freshmen (N = 1355), for example, 4.1% met a somewhat modified criteria for bulimia; this group consisted of 7.8% of the freshmen females and 1.4% of the males (Pyle, et al., 1986). In another study (Halmi, et al., 1981) of college students (N = 539), 13% of the respondents met the essential DSM-III criteria for bulimia, 87% of whom were female, which was 19% of the total sample of females who responded to the survey. However, the relationship between eating disorders and chemical dependency has not received as much attention.

ADOLESCENT CHEMICAL DEPENDENCY

The use and abuse of chemical substances by adolescents is an increasingly serious problem in this country. For example, Denoff (1987) refers to substance abuse as the most "pressing" and "problematic" condition confronting adolescents today. In the Gallup Youth Surveys, teenagers themselves identified drug and alcohol abuse as their biggest problems (Gallup, 1986).

Young people from every ethnic group, geographic region, and social class are using and abusing all varieties of drugs. America, when compared to other industrialized countries, has the highest rate of drug use among its school children. Teenage drug use is, for example, ten times greater in the United States than in Japan (U.S. Department of Education, 1986). The most commonly used drugs by teenagers include alcohol, marijuana, illegal prescription pills, and cocaine (Gold, 1986). In 1975, the University of Michigan's Institute of Social Research began surveying high school seniors across the country to determine patterns of cigarette, alcohol and other drug use (Johnston, O'Malley, & Bachman, 1988). They found that alcohol is used widely and often by high school seniors, with nearly two thirds of seniors reporting use of alcohol in the month prior to the survey (Johnston, O'Malley, & Bachman, 1988). The percentage of seniors reporting they had used cocaine in the last year was 5.6% in 1975, and that rate more than doubled (to 12%) by 1979, and in 1986 rose to 12.7% (Johnston, O'Malley, & Bachman, 1988). More than half of all high school seniors had some experience with illicit drugs, while more than 90% of those seniors had experience with alcohol (Johnston, O'Malley, & Bachman, 1988).

One of the greatest problems that confronts, in particular, Black adolescents is alcohol and drug abuse (Dawkins, 1986; Kelly, 1983; Wheeler, 1987). Data suggest that the dangers of alcohol abuse are especially devastating to the health of Blacks and that Blacks in drug treatment programs are three times more likely than Whites to be involved with lethally addictive drugs (Wheeler, 1987). Primary victims of chemical dependency appear to be Black urban youth (Dawkins, 1986; Kelly, 1985). Plagued by problems of school failure, unemployment, and family disarray (Dawkins, 1986; Kelly, 1985) Black urban youths are peculiarly susceptible to the easy escape and other enticements that drugs seem to offer.

Among Black urban youth, it has been found that 76% of those youth who reported that their first drink occurred before age 15 became regular drinkers between the ages of 13 and 18 and that heavy drinkers began drinking before age 15 (Dawkins, 1986). Early drinking occurred in social situations, with peer pressure influencing the tendency to become intoxicated from alcohol use, and that the most frequent times for drinking were holidays, weekends, and evenings (Dawkins, 1986). Black urban youth are consistently confronted with the decision of whether or not to engage in the use of alcohol and other drugs. It has been suggested that drinking alcohol, for example, can become a significant coping strategy for many Black adolescents who have little opportunity to observe more appropriate coping strategies because their parents, also overwhelmed with social conditions, sometimes turn to alcohol for solace and escape (Kelly, 1985).

EATING DISORDERS

Anorexia nervosa, bulimia nervosa, and compulsive eating are forms of eating disorders which, in recent years, have become increasingly more common (Bargman, 1983; Casper, Eckert, Halmi, Goldberg, & Davis, 1980; Halmi, et al., 1981; Katzman, Wolchik, & Braver, 1984; Mitchell & Eckert, 1987; Mitchell & Pyle, 1981; Pyle, et al., 1986). Fortunately, considerable progress has been made in understanding the biological disturbances (Brownell, 1984; Fairburn, Cooper, & Cooper, 1986; Johnson & Maddi, 1986; Laessle, Tuschl, Kotthaus, & Pirke, 1989), psychological issues (Laessle, Tuschl, Waadt, & Pirke, 1989; Williamson, Kelley, Davis, Ruggiero, & Blouin, 1985), and societal pressures (Chernin, 1981; Dickstein, 1988-89; Orbach, 1982) which contribute to these disorders. Considerable progress has also been made in assessment (Cooper, Taylor, Cooper, & Fairburn, 1987; Garner, Olmsted, & Polivy, 1983; Goldfarb, Dykens, & Gerrard, 1985; Hawkins & Clement, 1980; Johnson & Pure, 1986) and new, and also more comprehensive treatments have been developed (Connor-Greene, 1987; Fairburn, 1984; Foreyt, 1987; Foster, Thomas, & Brownell, 1985; Lenihan & Kirk, 1990).

Virtually every system in the human body can be affected by eating disorders. Some of the medical complications, such as poor temperature regulation, for example, may be relatively benign. However, other complications, such as cardiac arrhythmias, severe electrolyte abnormalities, and rupturing of the esophagus, may be life threatening. For example, the use of ipecac, a substance sold over the counter in pharmacies is particularly problematic in that it is directly toxic to the heart. Additional medical problems include hair loss, dental decay, palpitations, chest pain, esophagitis, constipation, loss of regular menses, diminished bone mineral density, and anemia. Fortunately, with proper medical treatment, these conditions are almost always reversible (Neuman & Halvorson, 1983).

Anorexia Nervosa

Anorexia nervosa is characterized by self-starvation; an intense fear of weight gain; a refusal to maintain normal weight for one's age and height; and, a distorted way in which one's body is perceived, commonly referred to as "body image disturbance" (Bruch, 1978; Chernin, 1981; Garner, Olmsted, Polivy, & Garfinkel, 1984). The American Psychiatric Association's (1987) *Diagnostic and Statistical Manual of Mental Disorders-Revised (DSM-III-R)* specifies diagnostic criteria for anorexia nervosa (DSM-III-R; 307.10). Female anorexics frequently experience loss of a regular menstrual cycle. Individuals with anorexia nervosa are determined to become thin and have an intense, irrational fear of becoming fat, both of which may often increase even as weight is lost. Anorexia is often the first phase of an eating disorder history.

Bulimia Nervosa

Bulimia nervosa is characterized by recurrent episodes of binge eating; a feeling of lack of control over eating behavior during binge episodes; the use of self-induced vomiting, laxatives, diuretics, strict dieting, or vigorous exercise to prevent weight gain; and, similar to anorexia nervosa, a persistent concern with body shape and weight (Boskind-White & White, 1983; Cauwels, 1983; Johnson & Pure, 1986; Lindholm & Wilson, 1988; Striegel-Moore, Silberstein, & Rodin, 1986). DSM-III-R specifies diagnostic criteria for bulimia nervosa (DSM-III-R; 307.51). It is a commonly held misconception that people are not bulimic if they do not self induce vomiting (cf., Polivy & Herman, 1985). The binge-purge cycle is typically followed by depressed mood, self-depreciating thoughts, and an awareness that the behavior is abnormal and out of control.

Compulsive Eating

Compulsive eating is characterized by overeating and eating during times when one is not necessarily hungry. Compulsive eating differs from bulimia in that there are no clear episodes of binge eating or purging. Rather, compulsive eaters describe eating frequently throughout the day and are aware that their eating is driven more by emotions than by hunger. The DSM-III-R category of Eating Disorder Not Otherwise Specified (DSM-III-R; 307.50) is used for this condition.

EATING DISORDERS AMONG ADOLESCENTS

The incidence of eating disorders seems to be increasing markedly in Western societies. There is some speculation that the number of people who are experiencing various versions of the syndrome has reached epidemic proportions (Bargman, 1983). This is particularly true among adolescents. The frequency of anorexia nervosa reported among adolescent girls averages about 1% (Lachenmeyer & Muni-Brander, 1988; Nylander, 1970; Pope, Hudson, Yargelun-Todd, & Hudson, 1984), while bulimia averages about 6% (Crowther, Post, & Zaynor, 1985; Greenfield, Quinlan, Harding, Glass, & Bliss, 1987; Gross & Rosen, 1988; Johnson, Lewis, Love, Lewis, & Stuckey, 1984; Lachenmeyer & Muni-Brander, 1988; Maceyko & Nagelberg, 1985; Pope et al., 1984).

Among adolescents the occurrence of eating disorders is associated with an array of other problems, not the least of which is chemical dependency. In a study of 86 White females, aged 13 to 21 years old, it was found that client's scores on the mood and dysregulation factor were significantly correlated with a childhood history of unhappiness, weight disorder, severe depression, abuse of alcohol and illicit drugs, disharmonious patterns of family interaction, and increased prevalences of obesity, alcoholism, and depression within another family member (Stober, 1983).

Some recent research has focused on the emergence of bulimic symptoms among individuals with no history of significant weight disorder. Studies have indicated that these individuals are predominantly single, White females, from 15 to 20 years of age, who are well educated, and of normal weight for their height; most of the women were involved in the bulimic behaviors on a more than weekly basis for approximately five and one-half years prior to their assessment (Johnson, Stuckey, Lewis, Love, & Lewis, 1982; Johnson et al., 1984; Mitchell & Pyle, 1981).

One study investigated the incidence of bulimia and related weight control behaviors among a predominantly (80%) White sample of American high school students, aged 13 to 19 years (Johnson et al., 1982). The results indicated that 52% of the young women had dieted by the age of 14 years and 14% were chronic dieters; binge eating episodes on a weekly or greater basis were reported by 16%; 4% reported using self-induced vomiting on a weekly or greater basis; and, 8% appeared to have bulimia nervosa (Johnson et al., 1982). Bulimia usually begins in late adolescence or the early twenties. The most frequent age of onset is said to be 18 years, a time when most people are under a great deal of pressure to make major life decisions and are in developmental transitions (Neuman & Halvorson, 1983).

Anorexia nervosa is, in the vast majority of cases, a disorder of adolescents, who are in a period of vulnerability to all kinds of problems. The most common ages for developing anorexia nervosa coincide with points of developmental transition. The 14 year old is often moving from junior high school to a high school setting, while the 18 year old is graduating from high school and going on to college or a career (Neuman & Halvorson, 1983). Only about 10% of anorexics are male, thus females afflicted with this disorder outnumber males nine to one (Anderson, 1981).

Anorexia nervosa is often viewed as a reaction to the stresses of puberty. For females, the hallmark of puberty is the physical development which results in an obvious change of shape and, of course, menstruation. Some have theorized that anorexia nervosa is caused by a rejection of approaching female sexuality and an attempt to ward off the physical development typical of adolescence, yet others contend that it is the entire role of being a woman which is being rejected (Neuman & Halvorson,

1983). Perhaps, becoming an adult woman may be perceived by some younger females as undesirable. For a female, becoming an adult may be viewed as a loss of status (Neuman & Halvorson, 1983). Two other potent cultural influences affect the increasing incidence of this disorder as well: a burgeoning concern with nutrition and physical fitness, and a national obsession with slimness and calorie counting (Neuman & Halvorson, 1983).

Studies on the incidence among adolescents of various eating disorders, in particular anorexia and bulimia nervosa, have been conducted in various Western societies. For example, research based upon a sample of 1,500 girls, aged 14 to 18 years, in both private and state schools in London, England, indicated that one in 120 girls suffered from anorexia, and one in 270 from bulimia (Szmukler, 1983). Among another British sample, the incidence of anorexia was reported as one in every 200 girls (Crisp, Palmer, & Kalucy, 1976). An investigation of dieting behavior and attitudes in an adolescent sample from Umea, Sweden, concluded that the disorder of anorexia existed in a severe form in about one out of 150 adolescent girls (Nylander, 1970).

When adolescents perceive their life to be managed and supervised by others, they may begin to search for means of experimenting with autonomy. The need to grow up, to become self reliant, and to feel adequate, capable, and worthy of respect is so strong that young people may reach out in socially unacceptable ways to fulfill this need. Some of the ways in which this can manifest itself may result in an eating disorder (Pratt, 1983). Female adolescents, underestimating or not realizing their own strengths and abilities, will search for ways to make themselves more acceptable, to feel better, and to find approval. They strive to be beautiful, often equated in American society with thinness, in an attempt to overcome feelings of inadequacy (Cherin, 1981). They may conceive of their own body shape and eating habits as the one thing in life that they can control. At the outset, at least, they will probably encounter no opposition or criticism. In fact, as they begin to lose weight, they may enjoy approval and support from peers, adults, and society in general (Pratt, 1983). Unfortunately, the progressive nature of eating disorders is insidious.

EATING DISORDERS
AND CHEMICAL DEPENDENCY

Chemical dependency, especially that involving alcohol, barbiturates, amphetamines, and cocaine, has been noted to be frequently associated with eating disorders, such as bulimia and anorexia (Beary, Lacey, &

Merry, 1986; Bulik, 1987; Gold, 1988; Hatsukami, Ekert, Mitchell, & Pyle, 1984; Jonas, Gold, Sweeney, & Pottash, 1987; Lacey & Moureli, 1986; Roth & Klein, 1990; Yeary & Heck, 1989; Zweben, 1987). Drug abuse and alcoholism have been noted to affect 25% to 40% of the bulimic population, as compared to 10% of the general population (Banaszynski, 1981). One study reported that bulimic women used alcohol for the purposes of avoiding the depression associated with the binge-purging, to relax, and to delay and/or prevent overeating (Pyle, Mitchell, & Eckert, 1981). Henzel (1984) found 33% of an anorexic sample were serious alcohol abusers.

The treatment literature available in this area emphasizes the importance of implementing a multifaceted therapy approach which deals with the various aspects of the disorders (Crisp, 1980; Garner, Garfinkel, & Bemis, 1982; Hedblom, Hubbard, & Anderson, 1981; Lucas, Duncan, & Peins, 1976). Goff (1983) theorizes that the two behaviors, chemical dependency and binge-purging, reinforce each other and, furthermore, even suggests that they combine to create a new and more destructive condition. Goff (1983) emphasizes the need to address both addictions in treatment, lest the client retreat further into one condition, when attempting to recover from the other. It has been found that both disorders may occur in the same individual either simultaneously or serially.

There is special need for attention to chemical dependency, as well as family history of chemical dependency, and affective disorders, in dealing with depressed eating disordered adolescent clients. There is, in this regard, significant suicide potential with the bulimic population (Neuman & Halvorson, 1983). It is therefore critical to discover and discuss the role alcohol or other drugs play in a client's eating problem, and to devise a plan for dealing with this involvement. Even for those eating disordered adolescents who do not abuse alcohol or other drugs, drinking and/or drugging often still plays a role in their eating behaviors. For some persons, a drink or two, or moderate use of another chemical, lessens their resolve to deal with their eating in a responsible way and this may even result in a binge. For other individuals, it can become a substitute for eating and a means of either avoiding a binge or of avoiding the guilt that is frequently associated with either a binge or fasting episode. Research indicates that cocaine and amphetamines are frequently used as a means of weight loss and/or weight control (Newman, 1990). Eating disorders, in short, have many common features with the addictive patterns of chemical dependency, and these shall be examined in the next section.

ADDICTION CONCERNS

The compulsive use of food or other substances has certain pleasure inducing properties, including the fact that it produces an initial state of euphoria. This euphoria seeking state may be, in fact, a natural part of the human condition (Weil, 1972). Unfortunately, this temporary euphoria is then followed by a negative emotional state and this post euphoric discomfort only gives further stimulus to the repetition of the earlier rewarding activity.

The novice user may begin the compulsive activity, whether the use of food or other substances, because of the pleasurable sensations brought about through the experience. The environment where these pleasurable feelings occur often becomes associated with an intense altered state of consciousness; the pleasure setting then becomes a composite of cues that stimulate craving for the original need satisfying activity. This pleasure seeking behavior generally becomes ritualized. However, the body adapts to this stimulation by reducing the potency of its effects. Consequently, there is an increased need for more of the mood altering activity in order to experience similar alterations of feelings and state of consciousness, particularly as tolerance is developed.

The chemically dependent individual's increasing tolerance to a drug is similar to the eating disordered individual's need to become progressively more rigid with respect to food (Roth & Klein, 1990). Eventually, the person is no longer motivated by the original sense of pleasure or need gratifying behavior, but the activity serves only to relieve the sense of despair and physical discomfort that is felt when the mood altering activity is not present. The person, as he or she becomes addicted, begins to experience loss of control, progressive deterioration of social, economic, and health functions. Finally, the chronic absence of positive feelings about self produces a dependency on the mood altering activity, whether the compulsive use of food or other substances (Milkman & Sunderwirth, 1987).

Commonalities of Etiology

As with other complex problems, there is rarely a single explanation for either an eating disorder or chemical dependency. Both eating disorders and chemical dependency generally arise from a combination of long-standing psychological, interpersonal, and social conditions. Feelings of guilt, personal inadequacy, depression, anxiety, and loneliness, as well as troubled personal and family relationships may contribute to the development of either an eating disorder or chemical dependency. American culture, with its unrelenting idealizations of individualism, thinness, and the "perfect body," can also be a factor (Cherin, 1981; Neuman & Halvorson, 1983).

There are some general commonalities of symptoms between individuals suffering from either chemical dependency or eating disorders. The person typically experiences uncontrollable self-destructive behavior, both personally and socially, and often exhibits an internal denial of the extent of the compulsive pattern. The person may fail to acknowledge either the current or future consequences of these behavior patterns. However, the deterioration of symptoms will continue to occur, unfortunately, until intervention is begun. A great majority of the families of such individuals, with either one or both of these disorders, are very affected and family members are often involved in one of the disorders themselves. Earlier family dysfunction has often played a key role in the development of these self-destructive behavior patterns and families almost always exhibit either pathological involvement or pathological distancing from the affected person (Humphrey, 1983; Minuchin, Rosman, & Baker, 1978; Stober, Salkion, Burroughs, Anderson, & Casper, 1982).

In general, the substance, whether food or other substances, is said to be used to repress feelings, block emotional pain, and fill the feelings of emptiness. These individuals tend to have poor boundaries, external controls, lack discipline, take little responsibility, and tend to be demanding, egotistical, and self-centered, whether they have an eating disorder (e.g., Brownell, 1984; Dunn & Ondercin, 1981; Etringer, Altmaier, & Bowers, 1989; Katzman & Wolchik, 1984) or chemical dependency condition (e.g., Blane, 1968; Brandenburger & Pursch, 1989; Cox, 1985; Schukit & Monteiro, 1988; Sutker & Allain, 1988). With respect to these apparent similarities, it is usually assumed that there is an inherent relationship between chemical dependency and eating disorders (Cooper, 1989; Levison, Gerstein, & Maloff, 1983).

Biopsychosocial Approach

The biopsychosocial approach is an expansion of the psychological-etiological perspective which focuses on the purpose and involvement of the maladaptive behaviors that comprise these disorders, whether eating disorders or chemical dependency. Kellam, Simon, and Ensminger (1983) proposed a model in which alcohol and other drugs are first used to reduce stress or to achieve desired emotional or interpersonal goals. Then gradually the individual becomes involved in using chemicals in order to attempt to control the negative physical, personal, and social effects of previous chemical use (Jones, 1968, 1971; Kammeier, Hoffman, & Loper, 1973; Marshall, 1979). This process involves the developing relationship between personality, expectations, and problematic chemical use. A similar model was proposed for eating disorders by Rosen and Leitenberg (1984), who found that behaviors which were initiated for apparently positive objectives, such as to achieve thinness, self-control, and drive, could lead to a physiological state that actually increases affective instability and leads to increased symptomology.

The biopsychosocial model has been proposed both for eating disorders (Johnson & Maddi, 1986) and for chemical dependency (Zucker & Gomberg, 1986). The model is based on studies which suggest that some combination of genetics, family environment, personality structure, and sociocultural groups account for the development of these disorders, whether an eating disorder or chemical dependency. This model provides an expansive framework for assessment, intervention, and treatment.

FAMILIAL FACTORS IN EATING DISORDERS

Familial predispositions for developing an eating disorder appear to exist. Family histories often reveal the presence of other conditions which are attributed, at least in part, to hereditary factors, such as alcoholism, diabetes, depression, and obesity (Kalucy, Crisp, & Harding, 1977; Neuman & Halvorson, 1983; Winoker, March, & Mendels, 1980).

Anorexics, for example, do tend to come from families which express concern over food issues (Minuchin, Rosman, & Baker, 1978; Neuman & Halvorson, 1983). This concern may be the result of special dietary needs of a family member, such as an emphasis on nutrition or previous struggles around controlled eating. The family may also have used food for purposes other than simple nourishment; eating may have been used when family members faced unpleasant problems, as a sign of love and caring for the providers, to fill time, or as a means to keep the family together. Some families, for instance, when confronting problems react to them by eating, while others will not eat when under stress; other families may require members to show their acceptance and love by eating food prepared for them.

Family and personal histories of weight disorder are also likely to influence the developmental conditioning for specific food preferences, approach-avoidance behaviors with regard to food, and reactivity to food stimuli, all of which might promote compensatory binge eating in response to the deprivation of anorexia (Stober, 1983). In a similar manner, the relationship of familial depression and alcoholism to bulimia in anorexic clients suggests that affective disturbances disinhibit dietary self-restraint and may be causally linked to limited personal control and low self-efficacy (Stober, 1983).

In some cases there may actually be more direct biological relationships present, particularly in clients with a familial risk for affective disorders (Stober, 1983; Winoker et al., 1980). Eating disordered clients whose family histories are riddled with affective disorders, including manic-depression and alcoholism, are quite common. These individuals may have, for example, a genetically transmitted brain function deficit that is only exacerbated by loss of weight and nutritional deprivation, perhaps by impacting on catecholamine functioning; a process that may produce anorexic symptoms (Stober, 1983).

Certain parental characteristics, including personality factors and chemical dependency, appear to be associated with eating disorders (Crisp, Harding, & McGuinness, 1974; Halmi & Loney, 1973; Stober et al., 1982). Mothers are often portrayed as dominant, intrusive, and very frequently as having periods of depression, while fathers, on the other hand, are described as generally aloof or passive. Alcoholism is, for example, often present in one or both parents, as is obesity or exceptional thinness (Neuman & Halvorson, 1983). For the parents of anorexic clients, distinct patterns of personality deviance, alcoholism, and family psychiatric morbidity have been found (Stober, 1981; Stober et al., 1982). In a similar fashion, it has been found that normal weight bulimics had a greater frequency of paternal obesity, while anorectic bulimics had a greater frequency of maternal obesity (Garner, Garfinkel, & O'Shaughnessy, 1983). Parents of bulimic anorexics also report greater marital discord and more emotional distance from their children (Humphrey, 1983; Stober et al., 1982). In addition, parental alcohol use, at a frequency of more than once a month, was almost twice as common among normal weight bulimics and anorectic bulimics than among the anorectic restricters (Garner et al., 1983).

Psychodynamic and family systems theorists (Bruch, 1973; Masterson, 1977; Minuchin et al., 1978; Selvini-Palazzoli, 1974; Sours, 1974) have proposed a familial source for anorexia. This has been conceptualized as the unprepared adolescent's response to demands during puberty for separation and individuation from overprotective and overly involved parents. In this regard, it has been found that fathers of bulimic anorexics scored higher on the MMPI indices of impulsivity, poor frustration tolerance, dissatisfaction with family relationships, irritability, as well as alcoholism (Stober et al., 1982). Furthermore, mothers of bulimic anorexics scored higher on MMPI measures of familial dissatisfaction, hostility, and depression (Stober et al., 1982). There is thus a significant familial contribution involved in the etiology of eating disorders.

OVERVIEW OF STUDY

The purpose of this study was to investigate whether the construct of eating disorders was associated with some chemical dependency factors, as well as satisfaction with life, and health locus of control of first-time Black students (N = 374) entering a medium-sized, public-supported, urban, eastern community college. The chemical dependency factors examined in this study were age of first use, frequency of use, and reported family history of chemical dependency; other factors examined were satisfaction with life, health locus of control, and eating disorders.

METHOD

Procedure

This study was conducted during the Freshmen Registration at an urban, eastern community college, which was an opportunity for incoming college freshmen to make initial contact with academic services and departments on campus. Cooperation with Registration staff assured control of the freshmen flow and continuous interaction with the new students. These new students were informed that the study was for programming and research purposes, and that all responses would remain confidential.

Instrumentation

The instruments used in this study consisted of a composite package including the Compulsive Eating Scale, Core Instrument, Health Locus of Control Scale, and the Satisfaction With Life Scale.

Compulsive Eating Scale. The Compulsive Eating Scale (CES) is an 8-item unidimensional instrument which measures compulsive eating (Kagan & Squires, 1984). The CES assesses one's inability to control eating behavior in terms of overeating and eating during times when one is not necessarily hungry. Scores range from 8 to 40, with higher scores indicating more compulsivity in one's eating. The CES was developed on a sample of over 2000 high school students and it has fair internal consistency with a Cronbach's alpha of .75 reported (Kagan & Squires, 1984).

Core Instrument. The Core Instrument (CORE) is an 87-item multidimensional instrument which is designed to assess the nature and extent of alcohol and other drug use and abuse at post-secondary institutions (Presley, Harrold, Scouten, & Lyerla, 1990). The CORE was developed by an Instrument Selection Committee of the Fund for the Improvement of Post-secondary Education (FIPSE) Drug Prevention Grantee Group in Higher Education to serve as a pre/post evaluation instrument that was uniform, comparable, and easy to use within program structures. The CORE can provide information about demographics and other student characteristics; drug use habits, such as age of first use, and frequency of use within the last year; and, family history of chemical dependency. The CORE appears to be a stable, reliable instrument. The test-retest correlations for age of first use items, for example, were relatively high, ranging from .61 to .99 (Presley et al., 1990).

Health Locus of Control Scale. The Health Locus of Control Scale is an 11-item unidimensional instrument developed to predict health related behavior in terms of locus of control (Wallston, Wallston, Kaplan, & Maides, 1976). Scores range from 11 to 66, with higher scores indicating a more external health locus of control. The construct of health locus of control is concerned with the perception that individuals have as to the cause of their health. It is held that knowledge of locus of control should theoretically contribute to the prediction of health behavior (Wallston, Wallston, & DeVellis, 1978). Individuals who perceive that their health is the result of luck, fate, chance, as under the control of powerful others, or as unpredictable, are considered to have external health control. Individuals who perceive that their health is contingent upon their behavior, or their relatively permanent characteristics, are considered to have internal health control. The HLC has fairly good internal consistency with a Cronbach's alpha of .72 reported (Wallston et al., 1978).

Satisfaction With Life Scale. The Satisfaction With Life Scale (SWLS) is a 5-item unidimensional instrument which measures subjective life satisfaction (Diener, Emmons, Larsen, & Griffin, 1985). Life satisfaction as a specific domain of subjective well-being, refers to the cognitive-judgmental aspects of general life satisfaction. The SWLS assesses an individual's judgement of his or her quality of life. Scores range from 5 to 35, with higher scores indicating more satisfaction with life. The SWLS was developed on a sample of 176 undergraduates and it has very good internal consistency with a Cronbach's alpha of .87 reported (Diener et al., 1985). In addition, the SWLS appears to have fairly high reliability with a two-month test-retest reliability correlation of .82 reported (Diener et al., 1985).

RESULTS

The respondents in this study were first-time, full-time Black college freshmen (N = 374) attending Freshmen Registration at that community college. Since Freshmen Registration was open to all entering freshmen and since only the Black students are considered in this study, the Black students who participated were a reasonable representation of the Black undergraduate students entering that community college. The average age of these Black students was 23.5 years (SD = 7.439). There were slightly more female than male respondents, 60% (n = 225) and 40% (n = 149) respectively. The average age of the female Black community college students was 24 years (SD = 7.923), while that of the males was 22.8 years (SD = 6.596). The majority (81.3%, n = 304) of these Black students were single, while 10.4% (n = 39) were married, 5.4% (n = 20) were separated, 2.1% (n = 8) were divorced, and 0.8% (n = 3) were widowed.

The mean score on the CES was 11.596 (SD = 4.763), with little difference by gender; females had an average CES score of 11.418 (SD = 4.754) and males averaged 11.866 (SD = 4.780). However, CES scores ranged from 8 to 35 and it therefore seemed reasonable to expect that some of this variability would be explained by chemical dependency factors, as well as health locus of control and satisfaction with life.

Age of First Use and Use Within Last Year

There were strong positive relationships, as is, of course, to be expected, between the age of first use and the current frequency of use for various drugs. For example, the correlation coefficient between the age of first use and the use within the last year of tobacco was .662. There was little difference by gender; there was only a slightly higher positive association for this particular relationship among males (r = .682), than there was among females (r = .650). Accordingly, 43.8% of the variability in use of tobacco within the last year among this sample of Black students could be explained by the age at which they first smoked.

The correlation coefficient between the age of first use and the use within the last year of alcohol was .542. Again, there was little difference by gender; there was only a slightly higher positive association for this particular relationship among males (r = .596), than among females (r = 527). Accordingly, 29.4% of the variability in the use of alcohol within the last year among this sample of Black students could be explained by the age at which they first drank alcoholic beverages.

The correlation coefficient between the age of first use and the use within the last year of marijuana was .417. There was considerable difference between genders in the strength of this particular relationship; among males there was a strong positive association (r = .558), while among females there was only a slight positive association (r = .316). Accordingly, 17.4% of the variability in the use of marijuana within the last year among this overall sample of Black students could be explained by the age at which they first smoked marijuana; while 31.1% of this variability could be explained among the males, only 9.9% could be explained among the Black females.

The correlation coefficient between the age of first use and the use within the last year of cocaine was .565. There was considerable difference between genders in the strength of this particular relationship, as there was for that pertaining to marijuana; while among males there was a very strong positive association (r = .721), among females there was only a moderate positive association (r = .374). Accordingly, 31.9% of the variability in the use of cocaine within the last year among this overall sample of Black students could be explained by the age at which they first used cocaine; while 52.0% of this variability could be explained among the males, only 14.0% could be explained among the Black females.

This sample has much lower drug use compared with national collegiate averages (Johnston, O'Malley, & Bachman, 1988). The Black community college students surveyed in this study, those entering college, are, by contrast with their peers, self-selected, upwardly mobile, individuals who are successfully coping by emerging from a difficult environment. Many of the respondents do suffer from codependency, as well as family, economic, and role stressors, however, they do not report the levels of chemical dependence that might otherwise be expected.

Eating Disorders

Surprisingly, very little to no relationship between eating disorders and chemical dependency factors was found. The CES scores demonstrated no particular relationship to the current frequency of use for various drugs, nor to age of first use. For example, there was almost no association (r = −.008) between the average number of alcoholic drinks consumed per week and CES scores. The correlation between the use of tobacco within the last year and CES was only .059, with little difference between females (r = .044) and males (r = .089); thus only .3% of the variability in eating disorders could be explained by frequency of tobacco use. The correlation between the use of beverage alcohol within the last year and CES was .030; thus only .09% of the variability in eating disorders could be explained by the frequency of drinking alcoholic beverages. The correlation between the use of marijuana within the last year and CES was − .018; thus only .03% of the variability in eating disorders could be explained by the frequency of smoking marijuana. The correlation between the use of cocaine within the last year and CES was − .006; thus only .004% of the variability in eating disorders could be explained by the frequency of cocaine use. Nor was the age of first use for these drugs related to eating disorders, whether for tobacco (r = .053), alcohol (r = .034), marijuana (r = .077), or cocaine (r = − .139). Family history of chemical dependency was also unrelated to eating disorders. The correlation between CES and positive family history was .094, with little difference between females (r = .074) and males (r = .118); thus only .9% of the variability in eating disorders could be explained by having a family history of chemical dependency.

There was also almost no association found among this sample of Black students between eating disorders and either health locus of control or satisfaction with life. The correlation between CES and HLC was .029, with only very slight differences between females (r = − .006) and males (r = .087); thus only .08% of the variability in eating disorders could be explained by health locus of control. The correlation between CES and SWLS was − .112, again with only slight differences between the females (r = − .191) and males (r = .027); and, thus overall only 1.3% of the variability in eating disorders could be explained by their satisfaction with life. Interestingly, there was also almost no association found between HLC and the frequency of use within the last year of either tobacco (r = − .013), alcohol (r = − .112), marijuana (r = − .076), or cocaine (r = − .124); nor between SWLS and the frequency of use within the last year of again either tobacco (r = − .022), alcohol (r = − .064), marijuana (r = − .034), or cocaine (r = − .002). There was, not surprisingly given the above findings, also no particular relationship (r = .052) between scores on the HLC and SWLS.

Black Adolescents

Since the average age (23.5 years) of the sample in this study was somewhat higher than that found in other studies of adolescents, it was also decided to look separately at those respondents aged 20 and under. It was found that 50% (n = 187) of the total sample was 17-20 years old, of which, more specifically, 40% (n = 75) were 17-18, 36% (n = 68) were 19, and 24% (n = 44) were 20 years old. This group was fairly equally divided by gender, 46.5% (n = 87) were male and 53.5% (n = 100) were female.

Interestingly, very little use of mood altering chemicals was reported by this group of Black adolescents. In fact, 82% (n = 153) reported that within the last year they had not smoked tobacco, 64% (n = 119) had not drank alcohol, 93% (n = 173) had not tried marijuana, and 100% (n = 187) had not used cocaine. Thus, for the purposes of analysis, there were very low levels of chemical use or dependency. Nor did there appear to be any other major differences between this group of Black adolescents and the total sample on the other measures examined. The average CES score among this group was 12.102 (SD = 5.805), and CES did not correlate strongly with the frequency of use within the last year of either tobacco (r = .017), alcohol (r = .061), or marijuana (r = −.015), nor with the HLC (r = .041), SWLS (r = −.109), or reported family history of chemical dependency (r = .103).

RESEARCH IMPLICATIONS

In general, these findings do not support the view that there is a relationship between eating disorders and chemical dependency. Among the sample of Black college students in this study, including the separate group of Black adolescents, no strong associations were found between eating disorders and the respective chemical dependency factors examined for tobacco, alcohol, marijuana, and cocaine, as well as reported family history of chemical dependency, nor satisfaction with life or health locus of control. However, it must be noted that the only assessment of eating disorders used in this study was a measure of compulsive eating and, had other instruments been used, the results may well have been different.

Nevertheless, strong correlations were found between the age of first use and the frequency of use within the last year of the various drugs examined. However, because of the reliance on self-report measures the validity of these results may be suspect since self-reported behavior is influenced by denial and, for chemical use particularly, either under or over-reporting of use. In addition, the results of this study may be generalizable only to Black college students, including Black adolescents entering college, and perhaps not to members of other ethnic and racial groups.

Consequently, additional research is needed to determine which variables and what specific conditions, if any, contribute to specific relationships between eating disorders and chemical dependency, as well as what sort of education and prevention programs are effective in influencing these factors. Further, additional research with more elaborate designs is needed to determine if chemical use and abuse is, in fact, a relevant issue to be considered, with respect to eating disorders. It is also recommended that other instruments be used, particularly measures of anorexia nervosa and bulimia nervosa, to explore possible relationships between eating disorders and chemical dependency. In addition, it is recommended that for further research clinical populations be utilized to initially document such relationships, where, if they exist, should be more pronounced.

COMMONALITIES OF TREATMENT

There are some general commonalities in the treatment of eating disorders and/or chemical dependency. The three primary levels of treatment consist of (1) outpatient, (2) intensive outpatient, and, (3) inpatient treatment.

At the first level of treatment the emphasis is on dealing with the underlying problems that contribute to the appearance of some eating disorder or chemical dependency behaviors. A short history of the problem is usually collected. Individual therapy is the primary treatment modality. Specific trigger situations are identified and coping strategies developed for acute, situational patterns of abuse.

The second level of treatment consists of intensive outpatient treatment. A contract is usually made with the patient who is motivated, has some support systems intact, and does not require inpatient treatment. Modalities include individual; group, such as Alcoholics Anonymous, Narcotics Anonymous, or Overeaters Anonymous meetings, and therapy groups; and, family therapy. This level of treatment is most suitable for patients with moderate problematic abuse because of the intensity of the compulsiveness.

The third level of treatment then consists of inpatient treatment. This level is designed for those with severe or chronic patterns of abuse. The objective is first for client stabilization and then on breaking the negative cycle of behavioral patterns. There must also be provisions for aftercare and adjustments made for leaving the structured, secure inpatient environment.

PRACTICAL SUGGESTIONS

There is much that can be done to help an individual who has an eating disorder and/or chemical dependency problem. First, collect relevant information about chemical dependency and eating disorders, and, in particular, identify local sources of treatment and support. Individuals should learn all that they can about alcoholism, drug addiction, anorexia nervosa, bulimia nervosa, and compulsive eating. Awareness undermines judgmental, mistaken attitudes about alcohol and other drugs, food, body shape, and compulsive behaviors in general. Whenever possible, discourage the notion that a particular chemical, diet, weight, body shape or size automatically leads to success, fulfillment and happiness. If an individual knows someone that he or she suspects has an eating disorder or chemical dependency problem, early action will prevent additional suffering. In a nonjudgmental and caring manner, tell the person of the specific eating disorder or chemical dependency behaviors that were observed and encourage him or her to seek qualified professional help. Intervention should also be predicated on the fact that what may have appeared to be a developmental crisis of the adolescent is, in actuality, also an interpersonal struggle and the therapeutic objective would also include changing the family as well as the adolescent.

Providing general knowledge to the school and community personnel, such as, for example, the school counselors (Price, Desmond, Price, & Mossing, 1990), about eating disorders and chemical dependency will help reduce the stigma and shame often attached to these syndromes. As more people become knowledgeable about eating disorders and chemical dependency adolescents will be identified earlier and referred to treatment. Directing the focus to one of teaching adolescents practical life skills, such as assertiveness, values clarification and decision making, will assist in the development of positive coping mechanisms to handle the difficulties of adolescence. This will help to deter them from using the avoidance and escape mechanisms provided by eating disorders and/or chemical dependency. By serving as positive role models for adolescents adults can show alternative ways to solve problems and, at the same time, teach self respect and responsibility. Any efforts to reinforce and teach adolescents to be assertive and responsible, as well as to support their attempts towards increasing their own self esteem and sense of confidence, will empower them to become all that they are capable of becoming.

CONCLUSIONS

From experience in working with chemical dependency and eating disorders, as well as a review of the literature (e.g., Neuman & Halvorson, 1983; Pyle, Mitchell, & Eckert, 1981; Roth & Klein, 1990; Stober, 1983; Yeary & Heck, 1987; Zweben, 1987), it is evident that an eating disorder may occur simultaneously with chemical dependence, it may precede the chemical dependence, or it may develop in early recovery from chemical dependence. They, in short, are two distinct forms of addiction that are also frequently associated. It is evident that students who are at high risk for developing eating disorders and/or chemical dependence have a family history of alcoholism, drug dependency, obesity, and/or affect disorder.

Adolescence is a period of particular vulnerability to all kinds of problems, including chemical dependency and eating disorders. Puberty is a period of physical development, that is associated with intimacy issues, risk taking, independence, and decision making, and is accordingly accompanied by a great deal of pressure to make major life decisions. There is no clear cut route to follow into adulthood. Assuming an adult role, with its accompanying responsibilities, may seem nearly impossible for a young person who is plagued with fears of inadequacy and who also has low self esteem. Adolescents, in general, and borderline adolescents, in particular, often experience intense feelings of abandonment (Masterson, 1972), as do, by the way, their parents (Reposa, 1979). The extent to which such feelings remain either a part of the normal process of adolescence or attain devastating proportions, including the manifestation of an eating disorder and/or chemical dependence pattern, for example, depends both upon the internal resources of the adolescent and those provided by family and significant others.

Adolescence is, therefore, a time of experimentation with varied coping mechanisms, including behaviors that may develop into either chemical dependence or an eating disorder. Whether adolescents are able to cope with the developmental crises of adolescence is dependent on both successful early childhood experiences, as well as the resources available at the critical points of development. Not only intrapsychic resources, but also those provided by the family for individuation and separation are important (Reposa, 1979). It is axiomatic that the more limited the resources available for coping, it is likely the more severe will be the problems of adolescence, including those of chemical dependence and/or an eating disorder.

Drinking alcohol, for example, can become a significant coping mechanism for many who have little opportunity to observe more appropriate coping strategies (Kelly, 1985). Research indicates that adolescents are at a high risk for developing eating disorders and/or chemical dependence (Crowther et al., 1985; Dawkins, 1986; Gross & Rosen, 1988; Pope et al., 1984; Pyle, Mitchell, & Eckert, 1981; Stober, 1983). It must also be recognized that adolescents may also be attempting to use their eating disorder and/or chemical dependence as a plea for help not only for themselves but for family members as well. This plea frequently takes the form of an action, such as an eating or chemical abuse episode, rather than of words, since generally during adolescence, feelings are communicated more by doing, than by saying. Thus, it is important to recognize not only the actions themselves but, more importantly, the messages that are being communicated by them.

The literature on eating disorders suggests that anorexia and bulimia frequently occur in adolescents between the ages of 13 to 19 years (Neuman & Halvorson, 1983; Pyle, Mitchell, & Eckert, 1981; Stober, 1983). It is further indicated that eating disorders most frequently develop among White, middle to upper class, female populations (Anderson, 1981; Crisp et al., 1976; Johnson et al., 1982; Mitchell & Pyle, 1981; Stober, 1983; Szmulker, 1983).

Little to no research has been done on the incidence of eating disorders among Black adolescents. Since the urban, Black adolescent is at high risk for chemical dependence (Dawkins, 1986; Kelly, 1985; Wheeler, 1987) and since chemical dependence has been noted by many to be frequently associated with eating disorders (Banaszynski, 1981; Gold, 1988; Henzel, 1984; Roth & Klein, 1990), it was felt that research needed to be done on the adolescent Black population to see if there were also high risk for eating disorders, which if unaddressed in chemical dependency treatment would make recovery more difficult. However, the sample of urban, Black students examined in this study did not report high levels of chemical dependence.

Research on White adolescent females suggests that the strong emphasis on success typical of Western societies is a causal factor in the development of eating disorders. Women formerly achieved their status through affiliation. Women took on the social status of the men in their lives, generally fathers first and then husbands. Today, new demands for independence, success, and sexuality confront women. These demands contradict other traditional demands that exist simultaneously. Women have been raised with traditional values and expectations which are now being challenged and modified. Thus, females find themselves caught in the "Superwoman" syndrome, carrying overwhelming and unrealistic expectations of themselves and trying to be all things to all people.

This research leads one to conclude that eating disorders may not be as prevalent for Black adolescent females, perhaps because the past ten years have not created a drastic change in the Black females' role. They have been acculturated for the "Superwoman" syndrome for generations, so there has not been such a drastic change in their values and traditional demands. However, one cultural influence on adolescent Black females that might foster eating disorders would be the obsession with calorie counting, slimness, and the burgeoning concern with nutrition and physical fitness (Neuman & Halvorson, 1983). Although, slimness, per se, has not been as highly valued by Black Americans.

In summary, no strong associations were found linking eating disorders and the chemical dependency factors examined in this study with the selected sample. Nevertheless, strong positive correlations were found between the age of first use and the frequency of use within the last year for tobacco, alcohol, marijuana, and cocaine. It is suggested that future research be directed towards other minority populations and also that other measures be utilized for assessing eating disorders.

REFERENCES

Anderson, A. (1981). Psychiatric aspects of bulimia. *Directions in Psychiatry, 14*, 1-7.

Banaszynski, J. (1981). Bulimia—self destructing victims use food for naught. *Minneapolis Tribune*, July 5, p. 7.

Bargman, G. (1983). Introduction. In *Understanding anorexia nervosa and bulimia*. Report of the 4th Ross Conference on Medical Research. Columbus, Ohio: Ross Laboratories.

Beary, M. D., Lacey, J. H., & Merry, J. (1986). Alcoholism and eating disorders in women of fertile age. *British Journal of Addiction, 81*, 685-689.

Bennett, W., & Gurin, J. (1982). *The dieter's dilemma: Eating less and weighing more*. New York: Basic Books, Inc.

Bilich, M. A. (1988-89). Demographic factors associated with bulimia in college students: Clinical and research implications. *Journal of College Student Psychotherapy, 3*, 13-25.

Blane, H. T. (1968). *The personality of the alcoholic*. New York: Harper.

Boskind-White, M., & White, W. C. (1983). *Bulimarexia: The binge/purge cycle*. New York: W. W. Norton.

Brandenburger, J. S., & Pursch, J. A. (1989). The faces of adolescent depression & chemical dependency. *Adolescent Counseling, 2*, 33-36.

Brownell, K. D. (1984). The psychology and physiology of obesity: Implications for screening and treatment. *Journal of the American Dietetic Association, 84*, 406-414.

Bruch, H. (1973). *Eating disorders*. New York: Basic Books, Inc.

Bruch, H. (1978). *The golden cage: The enigma of anorexia*. Cambridge, MA: Harvard Press.

Bulik, C. M. (1987). Alcohol use and depression in women with bulimia. *American Journal of Alcohol Abuse, 13*, 335-343.

Cahalan, D., Cisin, I. H., & Crossley, H. M. (1969). *American drinking practices; a national study of drinking behavior and attitudes* (Monograph No. 6). New Brunswick, N. J.: Rutgers Center of Alcohol Studies.

Casper, R. C., Eckert, E., Halmi, K., Goldberg, S., & Davis, J. (1980). Bulimia:

Its incidence and clinical importance in patients with anorexia nervosa. *Archives of General Psychiatry*, *37*, 1030-1035.

Cauwels, J. M. (1983). *Bulimia: The binge-purge compulsion*. Garden City, N. Y.: Doubleday and Company, Ltd..

Chernin, K. (1981). *The obsession: Reflections on the tyranny of slenderness*. New York: Harper and Row.

Connor-Greene, P. A. (1987). An educational group treatment program for bulimia. *Journal of American College Health*, *35*, 229-231.

Cooper, S. E. (1989). Chemical dependency and eating disorders: Are they really so different? *Journal of Counseling and Development*, *68*, 102-105.

Cooper, P. J., Taylor, M. J., Cooper, Z., & Fairburn, C. G. (1987). The development and validation of the Body Shape Questionnaire. *International Journal of Eating Disorders*, *6*, 485-494.

Cox, W. M. (1985). Personality correlates of substance abuse. In M. Galizio & S. A. Maisto (Eds.), *Determinants of substance abuse*. (pp. 209-246). New York: Plenum Press.

Crisp, A. H. (1980). *Anorexia nervosa: Let me be*. New York: Grune and Stratton.

Crisp, A. H., Harding, B., & McGuinness, B. (1974). Anorexia nervosa: Psychoneurotic characteristics of parents: Relationship to prognosis. *Journal of Psychosomatic Research*, *18*, 167-173.

Crisp, A. H., Palmer, R. L., & Kalucy, R. S. (1976). How common is anorexia nervosa? A prevalence study. *British Journal of Psychiatry*, *128*, 548-553.

Crowther, J. H., Post, G., & Zaynor, L. (1985). The prevalence of bulimia and binge eating in adolescent girls. *International Journal of Eating Disorders*, *4*, 29-42.

Dawkins, M. P. (1986). Social correlates of alcohol and other drug use among youthful Blacks in an urban setting. *Journal of Alcohol and Drug Education*, *32*, 15-28.

Denoff, M. S. (1987). Irrational beliefs as predictors of adolescent drug abuse and running away. *Journal of Clinical Psychology*, *43*, 412-423.

Diener, E., Emmons, R. A., Larsen, R. J., & Griffin, S. (1985). The satisfaction with life scale. *Journal of Personality Assessment*, *49*, 71-75.

Dickstein, L. J. (1988-89). Current college environments: Do these communities facilitate and foster bulimia in vulnerable students? *Journal of College Student Psychotherapy*, *3*, 13-25.

Dunn, P. K., & Ondercin, P. (1981). Personality variables related to compulsive eating in college women. *Journal of Clinical Psychology*, *37*, 43-49.

Engs, R. C. (1977). Drinking patterns and drinking problems of college students. *Journal of Studies on Alcohol*, *38*, 2144-2156.

Etringer, B. D., Altmaier, E. M., & Bowers, W. (1989). An investigation into the cognitive functioning of bulimic women. *Journal of Counseling and Development*, *68*, 216-219.

Fairburn, C. G. (1984). A cognitive behavioral treatment for bulimia. In D. M.

Garner & P. E. Garfinkel (Eds.), *Handbook of psychotherapy for anorexia nervosa and bulimia* (pp. 160-192). New York: Guilford Press.

Fairburn, C. G., Cooper, Z., & Cooper, P. J. (1986). The clinical features and maintenance of bulimia. In K. D. Brownell & J. P. Foreyt (Eds.), *Handbook of eating disorders*, (pp. 389-404). New York: Basic Books.

Foreyt, J. P. (1987). Issues in the assessment and treatment of obesity. *Journal of Consulting and Clinical Psychology, 55*, 677-684.

Foster, G. D., Thomas, A. W., & Brownell, K. D. (1985). Peer-led program for the treatment and prevention of obesity in the schools. *Journal of Consulting and Clinical Psychology, 53*, 538-540.

Gallup, G., Jr. (1986). Teens see alcohol/drug abuse as their top problems. *Alcoholism and Addiction/National Magazine, 6*(4), 13.

Garner, D. M., & Garfinkel, P. E. (Eds.). (1985). *Handbook of psychotherapy for anorexia nervosa and bulimia*. New York: Guilford Press.

Garner, D. M., Garfinkel, P. E., & Bemis, K. M. (1982). A multidimensional psychotherapy for anorexia nervosa. *International Journal of Eating Disorders, 1*, 3-46.

Garner, D. M., Garfinkel, P. E., & O'Shaughnessy, M. (1983). Clinical and psychometric comparison between bulimia in anorexia nervosa and bulimia in normal weight women. In *Understanding anorexia nervosa and bulimia*. Report of the 4th Ross Conference on Medical Research. Columbus, Ohio: Ross Laboratories.

Garner, D. M., Olmsted, M. P., & Polivy, J. (1983). Development and validation of a multidimensional eating disorder inventory for anorexia nervosa and bulimia. *International Journal of Eating Disorders, 2*, 15-34.

Garner, D. M., Olmsted, M. P., Polivy, J., & Garfinkel, P. E. (1984). Comparison between weight-preoccupied women and anorexia nervosa. *Psychosomatic Medicine, 46*, 255-266.

Goff, G. M. (1983). Bulimia: Status and considerations of health care. In P. A. Neuman & P. A. Halvorson, *Anorexia nervosa and bulimia: A handbook for counselors and therapists*. (pp. 43-61). New York: Van Nostrand Reinhold Company.

Gold, M. S. (1986). *The facts about drugs and alcohol*. New York: Bantam Books, Inc.

Gold, M. S. (1988). Eating disorders linked to chemical dependency. *Alcoholism and Addiction, 8*, 13.

Goldfarb, L. A., Dykens, E. M., & Gerrard, M. (1985). The Goldfarb fear of fat scale. *Journal of Personality Assessment, 49*, 329-332.

Greenfield, D., Quinlan, D. M., Harding, P., Glass, E., & Bliss, A. (1987). Eating behavior in an adolescent population. *International Journal of Eating Disorders, 6*, 99-111.

Gross, J., & Rosen, J. C. (1988). Bulimia in adolescents: Prevalence and psychological correlates. *International Journal of Eating Disorders, 7*, 51-61.

Halmi, K. A., Falk, J., & Schwartz, E. (1981). Binge-eating and vomiting: A survey of a college population. *Psychological Medicine, 11*, 697-706.

Halmi, K. A., & Loney, J. (1973). Familial alcoholism in anorexia. *British Journal of Psychiatry, 123,* 53-54.

Haskew, P., & Adams, C. (1984). *When food is a four-letter word.* Englewood Cliffs, N. J.: Prentice-Hall Press.

Hawkins, R. C., & Clement, P. F. (1980). Development and construct validation of a self-report measure of binge eating tendencies. *Addictive Behaviors, 5,* 219-226.

Hedblom, J. E., Hubbard, F. A., & Anderson, A. (1981). Anorexia nervosa: A multidisciplinary treatment program for patient and family. *Social Work in Health Care, 7*(1), 67-86.

Henzel, H. E. (1984). Diagnosing alcoholism in patients with anorexia nervosa. *American Journal of Drug and Alcohol Abuse, 10,* 461-466.

Humphrey, J. A., Stephens, V., & Allen, D. F. (1983). Race, sex, marijuana use and alcohol intoxication in college students. *Journal of Studies on Alcohol, 44,* 733-738.

Humphrey, L. L. (1983). A sequential analysis of family processes in anorexia and bulimia. In *Understanding anorexia nervosa and bulimia.* Report of the 4th Ross Conference on Medical Research. Columbus, Ohio: Ross Laboratories.

Johnson, C., Lewis, C., Love, S., Lewis, L., & Stuckey, M. (1984). Incidence and correlates of bulimic behavior in a high school population. *Journal of Youth and Adolescence, 13,* 15-26.

Johnson, C., & Maddi, K. L. (1986). The etiology of bulimia: Biopsychosocial perspectives. *Adolescent Psychiatry, 15,* 253-273.

Johnson, C., & Pure, D. L. (1986). Assessment of bulimia: A multidimensional model. In K. D. Brownell & J. P. Foreyt (Eds.), *Handbook of eating disorders.* New York: Basic Books.

Johnson, C., Stuckey, M., Lewis, L., Love, S., & Lewis, C. (1982). Bulimia: A descriptive survey of 316 cases. *International Journal of Eating Disorders, 2* 1-5.

Johnston, L. D., O'Malley, P. M., & Bachman, J. G. (1988). *Illicit drug use, smoking, and drinking by America's high school students, college students, and young adults 1975-1987.* Rockville, MD: National Institute on Drug Abuse.

Jonas, J. M., Gold, M. S., Sweeney, D., & Pottash, A. L. C. (1987). Eating disorders and cocaine abuse: A survey of 259 cocaine abusers. *Journal of Clinical Psychology, 48,* 47-50.

Jones, M. C. (1968). Personality correlates and antecedents of drinking patterns on adult males. *Journal of Consulting and Clinical Psychology, 32,* 2-12.

Jones, M. C. (1971). Personality antecedents and correlates of drinking patterns in women. *Journal of Consulting and Clinical Psychology, 36,* 61-69.

Kagan, D. M., & Squires, R. L. (1984). Eating disorders among adolescents: Patterns and prevalence. *Adolescence, 19,* 15-29.

Kalucy, R. S., Crisp, A. H., Harding, B. (1977). A study of 56 families with anorexia nervosa. *British Journal of Medical Psychiatry, 50*(4), 381-395.

Kammeier, M. L., Hoffman, H., & Loper, R. G. (1973). Personality characteristics of alcoholics as college freshman and at time of treatment. *Quarterly Journal of Studies on Alcohol, 34,* 390-399.

Kano, S. (1986). *Making peace with food.* Danbury, CT: Amity Press.

Katzman, M. A., & Wolchik, S. A. (1984). Bulimia and binge eating in college women: A comparison of personality and behavioral characteristics. *Journal of Consulting and Clinical Psychology, 52,* 423-428.

Katzman, M. A., Wolchik, S. A., & Braver, S. L. (1984). The prevalence of frequent binge eating and bulimia in a nonclinical college sample. *International Journal of Eating Disorders, 3,* 53-62.

Kellam, S. G., Simon, M. B., & Ensminger, M. E. (1983). Antecedents of teenage drug use and psychological well-being: A ten-year community wide prospective study. In D. Ricks & B. S. Dohrenwend (Eds.), *Origins of psychopathology: Research and public policy* (pp. 17-42). Cambridge, MA: Harvard University Press.

Kelly, J. (1985). Alcohol use and abuse among Black youth. *Health Education, 16*(3), 27-29.

Lacey, J. H., & Heck, C. L. (1986). Bulimic alcoholics: Some features of a clinical sub-group. *British Journal of Addictions, 81,* 389-393.

Lachenmeyer, J. R., & Muni-Brander, P. (1988). Eating disorders in a non-clinical adolescent population: Implications for treatment. *Adolescence, 23,* 303-312.

Laessle, R. G., Tuschl, R. J., Kotthaus, B., & Pirke, K. M. (1989). Behavioral and biological correlates of dietary restraint in normal life. *Appetite, 12,* 83-94.

Laessle, R. G., Tuschl, R. J., Waadt, S., & Pirke, K. M. (1989). The specific psychopathology of bulimia nervosa: A comparison with restrained and unrestrained (normal) eaters. *Journal of Consulting and Clinical Psychology, 57,* 772-775.

Lenihan, G., & Kirk, W. (1990). Using student paraprofessionals in the treatment of eating disorders. *Journal of Counseling & Development, 68,* 332-335.

Lindholm, L., & Wilson, G. T. (1988). Body image assessment in patients with bulimia nervosa and normal controls. *International Journal of Eating Disorders, 7,* 527-539.

Levison, P. K., Gerstein, P. R., & Maloff, P. R. (Eds.). (1983). *Commonalities in substance abuse and habitual behaviors.* Lexington, MA: Lexington Books.

Lucas, A. R., Duncan, J. W., & Piens, V. (1976). The treatment of anorexia nervosa. *American Journal of Psychiatry, 133*(9), 1034-1038.

Maceyko, S. J., & Nagelberg, D. B. (1985). The assessment of bulimia in high school students. *Journal of School Health, 55,* 135-137.

Marshall, M. (Ed.). (1979). *Beliefs, behaviors and alcoholic beverages: A cross culture survey.* Ann Arbor: University of Michigan Press.

Masterson, J. F. (1972). *Treatment of the borderline adolescent: A developmental approach.* New York: John Wiley.

Masterson, J. F. (1977). Primary anorexia nervosa in the borderline adolescent:

An object relations view. In P. Hartocolis (Ed.), *Borderline personality disorders.* (pp. 475-494). New York: International Universities Press.

Milkman, H., & Sunderwirth, S. (1987). *Craving for ecstasy: The consciousness and chemistry of escape.* New York: Lexington Books.

Minuchin, S., Rosman, B. L., & Baker, L. (1978). *Psychosomatic families: Anorexia nervosa in context.* Cambridge, MA: Harvard University Press.

Mitchell, V., & Bandell, J. (1983). Metabolic and endocrin investigations in women of normal weight with bulimia syndrome. *Biological Psychiatry, 18,* 355-365.

Mitchell, J. E., & Eckert, E. D. (1987). Scope and significance of eating disorders. *Journal of Consulting and Clinical Psychology, 55,* 628-634.

Mitchell, J. E., & Pyle, R. L. (1981). The bulimic syndrome in normal weight individuals: A review. *International Journal of Eating Disorders, 1,* 60-64.

Neuman, P. A., & Halvorson, P. A. (1983). *Anorexia nervosa and bulimia: A handbook for counselors and therapists.* New York: Van Nostrand Reinhold Company.

Newman, M. (1990). Study links eating disorders, substance abuse. *Newark Star-Ledger,* January 14, p. 12.

Nylander, I. (1970). The feeling of being fat and dieting in a schoolgirl population: An epidemiologic investigation. *Acta Socio-Medica Scandinavia, 1,* 17-26.

Orbach, S. (1982). *Fat is a feminist issue II.* New York: Berkley Publishing Corporation.

Ordman, M. N., & Kirschenbaum, D. S. (1985). Bulimia: Assessment of eating, psychological, and familial characteristics. *International Journal of Eating Disorders, 2,* 43-52.

Polivy, J., & Herman, C. P. (1985). Dieting and bingeing: A causal analysis. *American Psychologist, 40,* 193-201.

Pope, H. G., Hudson, J. I., Yargelun-Todd, D., & Hudson, M. S. (1984). Prevalence of anorexia nervosa and bulimia in three student populations. *International Journal of Eating Disorders, 3,* 45-51.

Pratt, J. (1983). Junior and high school. In P. A. Neuman & P. A. Halvorson, *Anorexia nervosa and bulimia: A handbook for counselors and therapists.* New York: Van Nostrand Reinhold Company.

Presley, C., Harrold, R., Scouten, E., & Lyerla, R. (1990). *Core pre/post evaluation instrument user's manual.* Minneapolis, MN: University of Minnesota.

Price, J. A., Desmond, S. M., Price, J. H., & Mossing, A. (1990). School counselors' knowledge of eating disorders. *Adolescence, 25,* 945-957.

Pyle, R. L., Halvorson, P. A., & Mitchell, J. E. (1986). The increasing prevalence of bulimia in freshman college students. *International Journal of Eating Disorders, 5,* 631-647.

Pyle, R. L., Mitchell, J. E., & Eckert, E. D. (1981). Bulimia a report of 34 cases. *Journal of Clinical Psychiatry, 42,* 60-64.

Reposa, R. E. (1979). Adolescent and family abandonment: A family systems approach to treatment. *International Journal of Group Psychotherapy, 29,* 359-368.

Rosen, J., & Leitenberg, H. (1984). Exposure plus response prevention treatment of bulimia. In D. M. Garner & P. E. Garfinkel (Eds.), *A handbook of psychotherapy for anorexia and bulimia*. New York: Guilford Press.

Roth, D., & Klein, J. (1990). Eating disorders and addictions: Diagnostic considerations. *The Counselor, 8*(6), 28-33.

Rowland, C. V. (1970). Anorexia nervosa: A survey of literature and review of 30 cases. *International Psychiatry Clinics, 7,* 37-137.

Ryser, P. E. (1983). Sex differences in substance abuse: 1976-1979. *International Journal of the Addictions, 18,* 71-87.

Schuckit, M. A., & Monteiro, M. G. (1988). Alcoholism, anxiety and depression. *British Journal of Addiction, 83,* 1373-1380.

Selvini-Palazzoli, M. (1974). *Self-starvation*. London: Chaucer Publishing Co., Ltd.

Sherry, P., & Stolberg, V. (1987). Factors affecting alcohol use by college students. *Journal of College Student Personnel, 28,* 350-355.

Steele, S. (1981). *How much is too much*. Englewood Cliffs, NJ: Prentice-Hall.

Steiner-Adair, C. (1988-89). Developing the voice of the wise woman: College students and bulimia. *Journal of College Student Psychotherapy, 3,* 151-165.

Stober, M. (1981). The significance of bulimia in juvenile anorexia nervosa: An exploration of possible etiologic factors. *International Journal of Eating Disorders, 1*(1), 28-31.

Stober, M. (1983). Subclassification of anorexia nervosa: Psychologic and biologic correlates. In *Understanding anorexia nervosa and bulimia*. Report of the 4th Ross Conference on Medical Research. Columbus, Ohio: Ross Laboratories.

Stober, M., Salkion, B., Burroughs, J., Anderson, A., & Casper, R. (1982). Validity of the bulimia-restrictor distinction in anorexia nervosa: Parental personality characteristics and family psychiatric morbity. *Journal of Nervous Mental Diseases, 170,* 345-349.

Stolberg, V. B. (1989). Alcohol consumption and attitudes among incoming freshmen college students. *Social Science Perspectives Journal, 3,* 161-170.

Stolberg, V. B. (1990). Health locus of control and alcohol-related factors among university students. *Social Science Perspectives Journal, 4,* 156-165.

Striegel-Moore, R. H., Silberstein, L. R., & Rodin, J. (1986). Toward an understanding of risk factors for bulimia. *American Psychologist, 41,* 246-263.

Sutker, P. B., & Allain, A. N. (1988). Issues in personality conceptualizations of addictive behaviors. *Journal of Consulting and Clinical Psychology, 56,* 172-182.

Szmukler, G. (1983). Weight and food preoccupation in a population of English school girls. In *Understanding anorexia nervosa and bulimia*. Report of the 4th Ross Conference on Medical Research. Columbus, Ohio: Ross Laboratories.

Temple, M. (1987). Alcohol use among male and female college students: Has there been a convergence? *Youth & Society, 19,* 44-72.

U. S. Department of Education (1986). *What works: Schools without drugs.* Washington, D. C.: Government Printing Office.

Vaillant, G. E. (1983). *The natural history of alcoholism: Causes, patterns, and paths to recovery.* Cambridge, MA: Harvard University Press.

Wallston, B., Wallston, K., & DeVellis, R. (1978). Development of the Multidimensional Health Locus of Control (MHLC) Scale. *Health Education Monograph, 6,* 161-170.

Wallston, B., Wallston, K., Kaplan, G., & Maides, S. (1976). Development and validation of the Health Locus of Control (HLC) Scale. *Journal of Consulting and Clinical Psychology, 44,* 580-585.

Weil, A. (1972). *The natural mind.* Boston, MA: Houghton Mifflin.

Wheeler, L. (1987). Promoting the health of Black Americans. *Black Issues in Higher Education, 4*(19), 1-3.

Williamson, D. A., Kelley, M. L., Davis, C. J., Ruggiero, L., & Blouin, D. C. (1985). Psychopathology of eating disorders: A controlled comparison of bulimic, obese, and normal subjects. *Journal of Consulting and Clinical Psychology, 53,* 161-166.

Winoker, A., March, V., Mendels, J. (1980). Primary affective disorder in relatives of patients with anorexia nervosa. *American Journal of Psychiatry, 137*(6), 695-698.

Yeary, J. R. (1989). Dual diagnosis: Eating disorders & psychoactive substance dependence. *Journal of Psychoactive Drugs, 21,* 239-249.

Zucker, R. A., & Gomberg, E. S. (1986). Etiology of alcoholism reconsidered: The case for a biopsychosocial process. *American Psychologist, 41,* 783-793.

Zweben, J. E. (1987). Eating disorders and substance abuse. *Journal of Psychoactive Drugs, 19,* 181-192.

The Adolescent Mentally Ill Chemical Abuser: Special Considerations in Dual Diagnosis

Hans H. Gregorius
Thomas S. Smith

SUMMARY. Chemical abuse in adolescence, in this object relations perspective, is predisposed by disintegration anxiety and by characteristic fears associated with status transitions. Severe manifestations of these anxieties and fears can also appear in the abuse of chemical substances and in psychiatric disorders. Because adolescence is a time of powerful external dependency (itself a function of incomplete psychological growth), the disease process associated with either chemical dependency or mental illness can be accelerated by the dynamics of the period. These dynamics are frequently controlled by sensitive dependence on such external sources as peer groups and by what are sometimes described in terms of the homeostasis processes of dysfunctional families. Dysfunctional families play into these dynamics in numerous ways—one way, for example, is by creating family crisis at the prospect of their adolescent children's growth and separation, which serve to convert their offspring into "problems" that then will serve the "family system" integratively. In general, such family "systems" discourage psychological growth by sustaining "enmeshment" of caregiving figures with their offspring. By contrast, external (nonfamily) adolescent milieus provide the adolescent with leverage against such dynamics as well as support in the face of isolation or repudiation. But since such external milieus are driven by conformist pressures, feed on separa-

Hans H. Gregorius, MD, PA, is Medical Director of Addiction Services at East Orange General Hospital in East Orange, NJ. He is a psychiatrist in private practice in Livingston, NJ. Thomas S. Smith, PhD, is Professor, Department of Sociology, Rochester University, Rochester, NY.

© 1991 by The Haworth Press, Inc. All rights reserved.

79

tion-individuation anxieties, and enclose rebellious and delinquent activities, they often encourage experimentation with retreatist and disinhibiting substances. In turn, abuse of these substances both telescopes the disease process connected with any underlying psychiatric problems and then superimposes on the signals of these illnesses additional chemically induced but transient symptoms.

YOUNG CHRONIC PATIENTS

Mentally ill patients under treatment for chemical dependence typically have a poor prognosis for recovery—poorer, that is, than chemically dependent persons without preexisting mental illnesses (McLellan, Erdlen, Erdlen, & O'Brien, 1981; Rounsaville, Dolinsky, Babor, & Meyer, 1987). Chemical dependence not only appears to aggravate such preexisting psychiatric conditions, but also from time to time to work in combination with them to produce what seem to be new disease entities altogether (Chatlos, 1989). Considered as a disease itself, chemical dependency's most pernicious characteristic is that, without treatment, it progresses irreversibly in stages to the point where its victims cope with the problems in their lives in immature, often inappropriate ways, eventually presenting signals of chemically-induced but transient mental dysfunction: psychotic thought, panic, depression, suicide, or other serious manifestations of personality disorganization. To students of this phenomenon, such signals have become familiar markers on the route untreated chemically dependent persons follow to death. When combinations of these signals make their appearance along with those of coexisting but different psychiatric diseases, appropriate diagnosis becomes a critical but difficult matter, especially when it comes to deciding upon optimal strategies for treatment and patient management.

This is especially the case of adolescents. For all of the physiological and social reasons making this period a turbulent stage of life, adolescence often appears to accelerate the progress both of mental illness and of chemical dependence. When added to either of these diseases, the characteristic stresses, dislocations, and growth of adolescence produce what has been described as "telescoping": a more rapid progression of the disease process (Morrison & Smith, 1987). When one combines all three conditions—adolescence times chemical dependence times mental illness, a truly pathogenic mixture is created; one which, has so often been noted in recent years, institutions and philosophies of health care in the United States are not designed to accommodate. Particularly with the deinstitutionalization of care for mental health in the United State, special problems of the adolescent mentally ill chemical abuser (MICA) have become increasingly evident. In the eyes of many acute observers, deinstitutionalization in the last two decades had produced a whole generation of what Pepper, Kirschner, and Ryglewicz (1981) describe as "young chronic patients": mentally ill young persons who have an excessively high prevalence of drug and alcohol abuse (Caton, Grainick, Bender, & Simon, 1989).

Just how prevalent this explosive mixture of conditions has become is, for obvious measurement reasons, difficult to estimate with precision (Schwartz, 1989). But the indirect indicators are profoundly foreboding. Some indication of the prevalence can be gauged from statistics on adolescent drug use alone. In national surveys of high school students conducted in 1987, according to Johnson and O'Malley (1988; cited in Bukstein, Brent, & Kaminer, 1989), estimates were that more than 90 percent had used alcohol at least once, fully five percent reported using it on a daily basis, and roughly 40 percent confessed to "heavy drinking" within two weeks of the date of the survey. How much of this heavy drinking is associated with mental illness is impossible to say, but findings from the National Institute of Mental Health's (NIMH) Epidemiologic Catchment Area (ECA) Program (e.g., Robins, Helzer, & Weissman, 1984; Myers, Weissman, & Tischler, 1984), the Isle of Wight studies (Rutter, Graham, & Chadwick, 1976; Graham and Rutter, 1985; & Rutter, 1986), and the Yale Family Study (Weissman, Wickramaratne, & Merikangas, 1984; Price, Kidd, & Weissman, 1987) all support the observation that "adolescence and young adulthood are important periods for onset of depressive (and other mental) illness(es)" (Christie, 1984). Indeed, although within the population at large rates of substance abuse are found among persons diagnosed as mentally ill (e.g., Alterman, Erdlen, & McLellan, 1980; Bergman & Harris, 1985; Davis, 1984; Fischer, Halikas, & Baker, 1975; Hasin, Endicott, & Lewis, 1985; Pepper, Kirschner, & Ryglewicz, 1981; Richard, Liskow, & Perry, 1985; Schwartz & Goldfinger, 1981), these rates are even higher among younger patients (Alterman et al., 1980; Safer, 1987) and among those who have been rehospitalized (Richard et al., 1985; Knudsen & Vilmar, 1984; Drake & Wallach, 1989). Across selected DSM-III-R categories, for example, the rates for alcohol abuse range between 7.1 percent and 48 percent, and for the abuse of other substances—narcotics, hallucinogens, barbiturates, stimulants, and marijuana—between 14 and 66 percent. First use for these drugs-of-abuse peaks in the age range from 15-19 years (Christie, Burke, Ragier, Rae, Boyd, & Locke, 1988).

Although studied with increasing frequency and subtlety in recent years, the problems of adolescent mentally ill chemical abusers can still profitably be reexamined through several perspectives. First, the category of the adolescent MICA itself needs rationalization in view of the heterogeneous nature of adolescence, particularly the important differences between its early, middle, and late stages. Second, in connection with such an exploration of adolescence as a category, the writer shall present "object relations" (a theory in which internalizing experiences result in internalized images) perspective geared to bringing into one theoretical framework several of the pertinent sources of variation useful in exploring relationships between chemical dependence and mental illness. Third, in developing this framework, it also will be useful to consider the variety of forms of dual diagnosis commonly reported for adolescent populations, and to consider these combinations in relation to adolescence itself. And, fourth, the issues related to differential diagnosis, prevention, and treatment will also be considered.

ADOLESCENCE AND THE MICA

As the Epidemiological Catchment Area Studies show (1988), the surface reason for an association between adolescence and various forms of dual diagnosis is that adolescence encloses the median age for the onset of important mental disorders—age 15 for anxiety disorder, 24 for a major depressive episode—as well as for various forms of chemical dependence—19 for drug abuse or dependence, and 21 for alcohol abuse and dependence. The lag periods separating the median age of onset for chemical dependence from the median age of onset for mental illness thus imply a degree of interdependence between these conditions. For some persons, as many studies have suggested, preexisting mental illnesses establish a risk of chemical dependence; for others, the development of chemical dependence contributes to the onset of mental illness. Not only are these two conditions thus mutually related as causes, but each appears to be independently predisposed by adolescence and its correlates.

Drugs and Prevalence Hypotheses

Since the prevalence of these conditions increases with the size of the adolescent population, increasing MICA concurrent pathology might have been expected to appear in the United States as a demographic "cohort effect," paralleling the movement of the "Baby Boom" through adolescence: Rates would therefore have peaked in the late 1970's, and thereafter stabilized at high levels—roughly following the trajectory of crime rates in the same period.[1] Measurement error and diagnostic fashions aside, this has not been the case. The prevalence of dually diagnosed adolescents dramatically increased in the 1980's and has continued to increase—an onset lagging behind the Baby Boom. Indeed, between 1986 and 1988 alone, roughly a decade after the cohort of Baby Boomers had departed the 14-24 year old age group, one psychiatric emergency service reported a 20 percent increase in dual diagnosis patients (Wolfe & Sorenson, 1989).

In view of this lag, the new and increasing prevalence of adolescent MICA's, as a purely numerical phenomenon, thus appears to be tied not to the number of adolescents alone but to changed circumstances in American life—circumstances that now appear as causes which interact with the inherent dynamics of adolescence to yield something new and unprecedented in adolescence itself: volatile, labile, difficult-to-diagnose-and-test combinations of mental illness and chemical dependence, unprecedented in American history on such a large scale. The obvious candidate as the prime cause for this phenomenon is not anything dramatically new about adolescence itself but the increased availability and use of drugs. Many other causes, as observers of adolescence have often speculated, no doubt play a role in producing the predisposition for drug abuse to culminate in dependence and for dependence to be associated with serious mental illness, but the prime cause of recent variations in the incidence of adolescent MICA is the prevalence of drugs themselves.

Drugs, Anxiety, and Adolescence

Adolescence as a Status Transition

Every adolescent engaged in separating from his or her "family of orientation" (Parsons, 1954) confronts developmental hurdles of psychological growth. These are typically made more difficult because they are compounded with stresses attending physiological maturation. In relation to the problems of chemical abuse and mental illness, the hurdles one needs to consider here include: consolidating a self-image, developing mastery strengths regarding control of the emotions, and establishing personal identity. Because these interrelated matters refer to strengths typically not carried over from childhood, adolescence is usually an anxious time—a phase of uncertain transition from childhood to adulthood, marked by all the marginality, contradiction, and "in-betweenness" of other status transitions. While life course theorists describe adolescence in many ways also characteristic of other status transitions, it is overcoming deficits and developing strengths of self-esteem and self-control that are among the classic hurdles for adolescent growth considered here (Blos, 1962, 1967).

Aside from underlying themes of physiological stress, adolescent anxieties take characteristic forms associated with counteracting forces normally at work in status transitions and specifically at work in developing and consolidating these psychological strengths. One set of forces, associated with growth and change, operated both to push adolescents out of their nuclear families and to pull them into the wider social world; the other set works to strengthen their resistance to such separation and to autonomy. Each of these forces is associated with underlying fears — firstly, the fear of domination, part of which is resentment against parental controls, and secondly, the fear of abandonment, part of which is insecurity over assuming responsibility for oneself in a complex and sometimes threatening world. Some of the more familiar themes in the study of adolescent "adjustment": substance abuse, sexual promiscuity, and criminal behavior, can be partly understood as patterns of "acting out" conflicts between these two underlying forces — between the need for security associated with the fear of domination, on the one hand, and the need for autonomy associated with the fear of abandonment, on the other. Other typical properties of adolescence are signals of how these two fears are somehow being managed (or mismanaged) developmentally. Familiar oscillations between attachment and rebellion, idealism and hedonism, impulsiveness and calculated manipulations, mood swings marked on the one hand, by boredom, depression, and isolation alternating, on the other, with anxiety, hypersociability, and demands for protection, exhibitionism alternating with voyeurism, all partly signal adolescent marginality and the developmental exigencies of the period (Davis, 1968).

Turbulence and "Sensitive Dependence"

One reason drug abuse can sometimes be interpreted as a matter of "adjustment" (or, alternatively put, as a form of "adaptation") is that, like so much else in the world of the adolescent, it often appears to be motivated by the need to bring anxieties and turbulent inner feelings under control. A familiar version of this argument is that adolescents use drugs to self-medicate themselves — to alter or control moods and feelings. While this is patently the case, it nevertheless remains true that there is something about adolescence itself that is at issue here in a causal sense — something that causes this period to be characterized by what shall be called "sensitive dependence": the condition in which small fluctuations in one of the environments of adolescent thought, feeling, or behavior produce large effects in others (Yalom, 1985).

Simply understood, sensitive dependence in adolescence is the vulnerability of adolescents to extreme feelings and to labile behavior—instability and turbulence produced by fluctuations in one or another environment in which development proceeds—physiological; psychological, interpersonal. In effect, small fluctuations get amplified out of proportion to their size, as they are transmitted from one system to another. Petty interpersonal rebukes strike the adolescent as devastating assaults on self-esteem; smiles from others as triggers for romantic idealization; repudiations by significant others as precipitators of suicide. Adults are generally less subject to the same turbulence because they possess psychological and interpersonal resources enabling them to bring their own feelings under control—to damp the effects within themselves arising from the causes of turbulence in adolescents. The resources associated with the capacity to damp and control feelings are often described in theory as "psychological strengths," and in certain theories they more specifically denote coherent schemata and cultural resources, on the other, associated with self-control and self-management. Developmentally speaking, such strengths are products of psychological growth and education; indeed, they are measures of growth and education. Functionally speaking, they amount to substitutes for caregivers—the "objects" appropriated to serve a caregiving function, the child introjects (i.e., forms schemata of, learns, etc.) during the course of its growth. These psychological structures are where the child then locates the strengths and direction to do for itself what it had formerly relied on caregivers to do for it (Blos, 1962; Kohut, 1984).

The adolescent without these capacities—who has "deficits" of self-esteem and self-control—has not developed psychologically to the point where, apart from continued reliance on caregivers for help, he or she is able to manage feelings and other aspects of personal life. The effect of being without these strengths—without what Kohut (1971, 1977) called the capacity to produce "coherence" in self—is to make adolescents externally dependent on others—or, significantly, on such substances and practices as they might utilize in order to produce in themselves substitutes for coherence. A coherence-substitute, in this sense, often amounts to a "different" feeling or subjective experience from the one the adolescent seeks to replace—for example, a subjective "difference" able to override the anxieties (Kohut called them "disintegration anxieties") that arise from dysphoric subjective experiences of incoherence in self or from fears occasioned by "withdrawal" from the nuclear family. From this "object relations" point of view, therefore, external dependency on others can be equated with external dependency on substances: both are driven by the same needs to control feelings, particularly to control the characteristic fears of domination or abandonment of this period, along with anxieties of disintegration.

How adolescents feel in these respects, significantly, is typically a function of the structures they rely upon to regulate themselves. Some regulators, such as responsive friends or caregiver-substitutes like teachers, are those an adolescent can usually rely upon to be closely adapted to his or her needs and wants; others, such as drugs or chemicals, are nonoptimal regulators and typically produce only short-term states of subjective euphoria, brought on by changes in brain chemistry, that are unable to eliminate (and indeed may deepen) the long-term psychological deficits underlying chronic sensitive dependence, fear, and anxiety. Clearly, the child whose dependence is on an empathic friend or caregiver, and who relies on such a person to develop insight and control over anxious feelings, has a better chance to grow psychologically to the point of being able to handle the same functions alone than does the child who turns to alcohol or drugs (Needle, 1986).

While a full consideration of the theoretical sources and implications of this kind of thinking is beyond the scope of this paper, it is important to indicate here that the basic pattern of reasoning presented is consistent with much that is known both about adolescence and about chemical abuse.[2] Moreover, the basic theoretical model is general enough to remain amenable to detailed empirical specification in the light of other variables and relationships with a role in these processes. One way to suggest how this is possible, without undertaking a thorough review of the detailed literature on adolescence and related themes, is to summarize and expand the argument in the open-ended way appearing in Figure 1.

Figure 1 depicts a functional relationship between "personal organization and functioning," on the one hand, and "family organization and functioning," on the other, along with a list of empirical variables on which each of these complex considerations is dependent causally, as described at various places in the sociological and psychological literature on families, chemical dependence, and personal development. What it suggests is that both personal and family functioning are each hypothetically affected by such exogenous considerations as social class, ethnicity, sex, genetic variables, age, and other considerations familiar from this literature. Family properties such as the division of labor between husbands and wives, for example, vary by social class and ethnicity; in turn,

FIGURE 1. Hypothetical Relationship of Personal Functioning to Family Functioning, as Affected by Various Other Causes

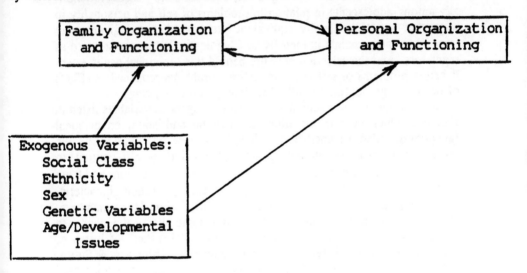

these properties of family organization tend to have effects on the socialization and mental health of children. (Disorganized families, thus tend to produce disorganized children.) More generally, there is a "functional" relationship between family functioning and the functioning of children — with dysfunctions in either area tending to produce dysfunctions in the other.

Figure 2 expands the argument by suggesting, as argued above, that "problems" in self and personality (as amplified by sensitive dependence and other correlates of incomplete psychological growth) are functionally related to chemical abuse. Chemical substances might have functioned as "regulators" for dysphoric feelings and other aversive subjective phenomena. In this version of the argument, chemicals are "used" functionally among adolescents in relation to problems of self and personality in ways that are "functionally equivalent" to how their caregivers were "used" at earlier points in their lives. Chemicals, that is, are selected as regulators. And the selection pressure behind this functional use is established in problems of self and personality — problems produced as effects of flawed or non-optimal family functioning and caregiving.

Again, implicit but assumed are the same exogenous variables listed in Figure 1 which operate as influences, beyond childhood, on personal functioning. Also assumed here although likewise left implicit are the respects in which other external regulators, beyond drugs, also continue to work during adolescence either to damp or amplify the anxieties and fears of the period. In particular, peer groups, depending on their characteristics, have powerful effects on the stability or instability of their members. Obviously as well, the many important insights into chemical dependence produced by family systems theorists (Stanton, 1979) that, for instance, chemical dependence is typically a "family disease" (Morrison & Smith, 1987) — can be incorporated into this model (although left undiscussed here) by expanding the concept of "family functioning."

Figure 2 also carries the argument one stage further. Here, the disease process has been "telescoped" by adolescence, so that mental illness is related functionally to chemical dependence. MICA seriousness is represented here by placing an arrow at the side of this diagram, pointed from the bottom to the top, describing a trajectory of increasing "severity" of mental illness and chemical abuse problems.

In no way does this functional representation diminish the potential autonomy either of chemical dependence as a disease or of mental illness as a disease. Either may occur without the other and each establishes vulnerability to the other. The generalized causal scheme appearing in

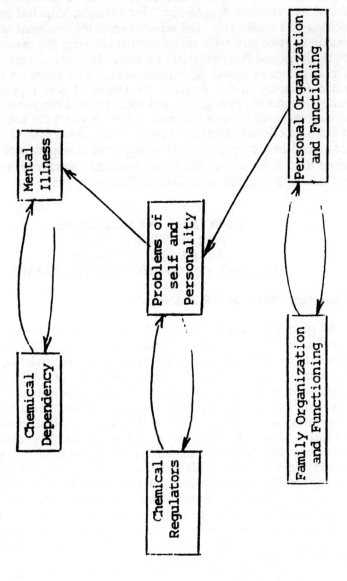

FIGURE 2. How Problems of Self and Personality, with Roots in Family Functioning, are Related Functionally to Chemical Abuse

Figures 1-2 is meant to preserve the peculiar sensitivity of the mental illness-chemical dependence relationship to other variable associated with adolescent "sensitive dependence." For example, hormonal changes associated with adolescence, and hence much of the emotional distress and sensitivity associated with sexual maturation, enter the diagram as the effects of age and developmental exigencies. Similarly, though the effects of peer groups in promoting experimentation with drugs are not represented explicitly in this diagram, the effects of peer dependence are readily introduced: peer groups and other external structures on which adolescents become dependent serve as milieus which can either mediate or damp the effects of preexisting problems in self and personality. Gangs and other delinquent peer groups typically serve as amplifiers of predispositions to experiment with drugs, and sometimes sources of the anxieties that motivates drug use itself (Short & Strodbeck, 1965).

CONCOMITANT VARIABLES
FOR MENTAL ILLNESS
AND CHEMICAL ABUSE:
SEVERITY OF PSYCHIATRIC PROBLEMS

Adolescent "General Life Problems"

Not specific psychiatric diagnoses but severity of psychiatric problems, according to McLellan, Erdlen, Erdlen and O'Brien, (1981), best predict treatment failure for dually diagnosed persons. In reconsidering this finding, Stoffelmeyr, Benishek, Humphreys, and Mavis, (1989), on the basis of their own and other studies, argue that poor prognoses in these cases may result from the effects, on coexisting psychiatric and substance abuse problems, of what they call "general life problems." If severity of illness but specific diagnosis contributes to poor prognosis, they reason, it may be because severity is itself caused by, and in turn amplifies, a person's problems in other areas of life — chronic unemployment, marital instability, legal problems, poor interpersonal relationships, high levels of dependence, etc. "Persons who rank high on psychiatric problems," they report, "also function poorly in many other life areas . . . [and] are characterized by the primary or 'extrinsic' (Wing, 1978) handicaps of poverty, poor education, lack of vocational skills, and marginal social relations (Stoffelmeyr, et al., 1989, p. 150).

Among adolescents, an equivalent phenomenon arises in relation to sensitive dependence. Adolescence itself, as we have seen, is often discussed with reference to what are thought to be analogous "general life problems"—if not exactly equivalent problems, problems nonetheless. Under this reasoning, severity of adolescent psychiatric symptoms, if not specific diagnosis, may well vary, as among adult patients, in relation to such general life problems—poor adjustment to school, unstable family relationships, interpersonal difficulties, delinquency problems, and high levels of dependence. Coexisting substance abuse, even when it dependently produces psychiatric symptoms, can also be caused (apart from preexisting liabilities) by the same general life problems. And, in turn, each of these effects then works to increase general life problems. Sensitive dependence sets up this unstable pattern of causation, as it is represented in general terms in Figure 2.

While severity may be the important variable affecting prognosis, the phenomena of concurrent pathology themselves can still be illustrated in relation to specific diagnostic categories. Before one considers in more detail the causal dynamics research on the subject illustrates, some of the typical patterns of dual diagnosis among adolescent MICAs will be considered.

Anxiety Disorder

Anxiety disorders are the most prevalent disorders in the United States and it is estimated that 25 percent of the population suffer from anxiety disorders of one type or another. Nearly 25 percent have accompanying substance abuse or dependence. A number of studies support coexistence of substance dependence and anxiety disorder including the phobic disorder, panic disorders, agoraphobia and generalized anxiety disorders (Weiss & Rosenberg, 1985). However, the existence of anxiety disorders and substance abuse in adolescence has not been carefully studied except for some family studies. Johnston and O'Malley (1986) indicated in a self report questionnaire about drug use that 41 percent of U.S. high school seniors who responded gave the reason "to relax or relieve tension" for their drug use. Significantly, the majority of these were users of sedatives or sedative hypnotics. Certainly social anxiety is a common finding in the adolescent population and is also a common report of adult alcoholics when they state that the first time they had a drink was the first time they felt like others or socially uninhibited. To feel relaxed and more adequate in a peer setting is a common reason adolescents give for the use of mood altering substances. For the individual who has a bonafide phobic disorder, panic disorder, or other anxiety disorder, it is again important to differentiate this not only from other psychiatric conditions but from a prolonged withdrawal syndrome.

It is also important to note that medications are available for these conditions which are not mood altering. Nevertheless benzodiazapines such as Valium and Xanax continue to be medications primarily prescribed for anxiety disorders by physicians. These must be avoided because of the danger of abuse and dependence as well as the potential for relapse to the substance dependent individual's drug of choice. In addition, there are a variety of treatments available including those of behavioral therapy which have proven to be effective without the use of medication. Odds are three times greater that previous sufferers from panic disorders will have a substance abuse or dependence problem as well. Epidemiological Catchment Area researchers discovered that mental illness prevalence rates are twice as high for those in substance abuse treatment programs versus substance abusers who have not sought treatment. That is to say about 55 percent also have concurrent pathology for mental illness in treatment versus about 24 percent in untreated substance abusers.

The NIHM and ECA study (Christie et al., 1988) is a multi year project in which researchers at four sites in collaboration with NIMH surveyed approximately 20,000 individuals. Ignoring a mental disorder in an identified substance abuser, or conversely not identifying or searching for substance abuse or dependence in the person suffering from a mental illness is a potentially critical oversight with potentially lethal effects. Evidence of dual diagnosis which exists in these individuals requires that both must be addressed and explored in order to formulate an appropriate treatment plan and consequent better clinical results.

Schizophrenia

The closeness with which drug abuse simulates classic paranoid psychosis has provided an important model for schizophrenia (Cloninger, 1987; Castellani, Petrie, & Ellinwood, 1985). As Bukstein and colleagues (1989) point out, "Pattern-specific drug use..(by) schizophrenic patients may eventually provide clues to underlying neuropathological mechanisms in the development and maintenance of schizophrenia." (Cf. Vingelis & Smart, 1981).

Drug-induced psychotic symptoms are also regularly reported in connection with abuse or withdrawal from stimulants, hallucinogens, cannabis, and phencyclidine. High doses of cocaine, for instance, produce a toxicity that manifests itself in hallucinatory psychosis (as for example, in phenomenon of "cocaine bugs") and subsequently in schizophrenia-like psychosis (Forno, Young, & Levitt, 1981) infused by paranoid delusions.

Preexisting schizophrenia is also of course a powerful risk factor for the subsequent development of substance abuse disorders of numerous kinds, a fact that often created difficulties when symptoms of psychosis are mistakenly diagnosed as drug-induced and the prescribed "treatment" includes detoxification.

Affective Disorder

Depression, Suicide and Substance Abuse

Suicide remains the second leading cause of death among adolescents. Approximately 60 percent of suicides occur in young adults and adolescents. Though the suicide rate among adults appears to have leveled off, unfortunately suicide among children and adolescents continues to increase year after year. Garfinkel (1987) in his article on adolescent suicide indicated that the suicide rate for high school students had increased 60 percent in Minnesota in the two years prior to his article. He also notes that this is not the highest rate in the country but that it is typical. He further notes that in a survey of over 16,000 high school students, for every completed suicide, there were over 350 attempts which translated into three out of every 100 high school students having made a suicide attempt within the preceding four weeks. Significantly, he indicated that 37.5 percent of the attempts are drug related. Though there are multiple risk factors, substance abuse is one. Another risk factor, of course, is depression and previous suicide attempts.

Schrier (1989) indicated that intervention should include: (1) the constant awareness of the possibility of depression and suicide in adolescents, (2) the availability of the treating individual on a 24 hour basis, (3) routinely ask questions about suicidal thoughts or attempts, (4) take any threat seriously, (5) evaluate intent and risk of occurrence, (6) avoid being judgmental in lecturing or moralizing, and take a positive approach which includes a look at options, (7) be certain that a referral is followed up, and (8) if antidepressant medication is warranted, know that it is potentially lethal if used as a means to terminate one's own life. Clearly the adolescent who suffers from a substance abuse problem as well as a coexisting psychiatric disorder is a high risk.

An important example of the effects of sensitive dependence in adolescence arises in relation to so-called affective disorders — those chronic disorders of mood and subjective self-report associated characteristically with depression and low self-esteem, and enclosing phenomena extending into diseases such as bipolar disorder and related manifestations of mood instability that occasionally culminate, especially among adolescents, in suicide or in chronic suicidal ideation.

Probably no psychiatric conditions associated with chemical abuse have been studied more than affective disorders. Depressive symptoms associated with chemical abuse, of course, are often a byproduct of chemical dependency itself. The dysphoria typically reported in conjunction with chronic alcohol abuse is a common example. Such research, however, has also shown that preexisting depressive symptoms must also be recognized as risk factors associated with the onset and maintenance of substance abuse (e.g., Braught, Brakarsh, & Follingstad, 1973). Supporting the same conclusion is the work of Deykin, Levy, and Wells, (1987), which shows that alcohol or substance abuse among college students is almost always preceded by the onset of major depression. Likewise reported data from NIHM Catchment Area Program show that the risk of drug abuse doubled for adolescents who had experienced the early onset of a major depressive episode (Christie et al., 1988).

As is also the case in relation to other psychiatric illnesses, treatment outcomes in this area are dependent on differentiating primary affective disorders from those secondary to substance abuse. When alcohol abuse is the primary problem, for example, medication is useless in treating depressive symptoms. Preexisting psychiatric illness by contrast, will often affect the course of substance abuse itself in numerous ways—for example, by increasing overall impairment and diminishing treatment compliance.

Conduct Disorder
and Antisocial Personality Disorder

Aside from the association of conduct disorder to other predisposing conditions of chemical abuse, such as ADHD, conduct disorder may also appear as one of the early manifestations of various incipient forms of mental illness. Developing during childhood and adolescence, it is a significant predictor of the onset of adult antisocial behavior in its more florid forms (such as full-fledged antisocial personality disorder) as well as occasionally serving to signal liability to other adult mental diseases such as schizophrenia. For all of the reasons predisposing persons with these other psychiatric conditions to chemical abuse, therefore, those with some tendency to conduct disorder are also likely to turn toward chemical abuse. During adolescence, especially, conduct disorder is also motivated by peer dependencies used both to modulate fears of abandonment and to weaken fears of domination. In such contexts, conduct disorder may appear as a consequence of conformist pressures or as a carryover of childhood exhibitionism. Conduct disorder that during childhood was understandable as an exhibitionist signal of mirroring "merger demands" directed towards caregivers—symptoms, in Kohut's (1984) sense, of psychological deficits, manifested as chronic tendencies to recapitulate caregiver-infant interaction, aimed at building psychological structure—also becomes during adolescence a way of "acting out" the natural conflicts of the period between underlying needs for nurturance and protection and needs for respect and autonomy, or between needs for love and status.

Although substance abuse can also be a "risk factor" in the development of conduct and antisocial personality disorder, part of the observed association between the two (Bukstein et al., 1989) is a matter of classification: substance abuse is a diagnostic criterion for antisocial personality disorder. Ingestion of disinhibiting drugs-of-abuse like alcohol or other chemicals "lowers the threshold for antisocial behavior" (Bukstein et al., 1989). Criminologists and others, observing changes in drug use in the last several decades, have speculated that a significant fraction of the increase in violent crime in the United States since 1960 is a function of the increased association between antisocial behavior and drug abuse, especially among adolescents (Silberstein, 1978). Investigating whether there is a direct causal relationship between drug abuse and violent crime, many studies have presented evidence showing the causal dependence on antisocial behavior on substance abuse, especially abuse of alcohol. The literature at this point is enormously complicated, though there is very little question about the association between alcohol and violent crime (Wilson & Herrnstein, 1985).

Numerous relationships between ingesting drugs and subsequent aggressive behavior have also long been established by important animal studies, many of which have provided models of drug abuse in rats and monkeys relevant to understanding human psychopharmacology. In unlimited supply, for example, cocaine is apparently so self-rewarding that animals will self-stimulate themselves until they are dead—an effect also observed in the behavior of cocaine-dependent humans. Persons under the control of this drug have severely impaired reality-testing, and when controlled by the symptoms of withdrawal, they become paranoid, experience attacks of panic, feel violent, hallucinate, physically injure others, are tormented by suicidal ideation and often attempt suicide. (Washton & Tatarsky, 1984).

Prison samples were startling. The coexistence of mental illness and substance abuse or dependency was 81 percent. Those prisoners with already identified mental illnesses have a rate of 90 percent. The etiological mechanism and causal relationship of these extremely high concurrent pathologies remains unknown (Christie et al., 1988).

Borderline Personality Disorder

A defining characteristic of the borderline patient is attachment behavior marked by vacillation between loving and hating. While Kernberg (1975) explained this behavior as a function of the borderline patient's reliance on primitive ego defenses such as intrapsychic splitting, others have explained the same behavior by focussing on interpersonal considerations. Arguing in this tradition, Melges and Schwartz (1989) suggest that typical oscillatory symptoms in the borderline patient's attachment behavior can be explained by positing that coexisting underlying fears equivalent to those argued above are inherent in all status transitions. The underlying problem for the borderline patient is "distance regulation": getting close to others raises fears of domination, whereas detaching from partners raises fears of abandonment. These coexisting fears—"regardless of whether the patient moves closer to or away from other people"—drive borderline patients along a path alternating between attachment and disengagement (Melges & Schwartz, 1989).

Another way of putting this is to say that borderline patients are chronically marked by an extreme form of sensitive dependence, a characterization Melges and Schwartz specify with Schopenhauer's story of porcupines on a cold day: at first huddling together to ward off the cold, they are driven apart by their quills, only later to be forced together again by the cold, whereupon they repeat the same cycle ad infinitum. Too much or too little distance is equally threatening to such prickly types (p. 115-116). Perhaps for this reason, as Morrison and Smith (1987, p. 473) observe, an important diagnostic criterion for borderline personality disorder is "impulsivity" or "unpredictability" in at least two potentially self-damaging areas involving addictive behavior ("e.g., spending, sex, gambling, substance abuse, shoplifting, overeating, physically self-damaging acts"). Thus, borderline adolescents reportedly abuse a wide range of substances (marijuana, alcohol, LSD, amphetamines, barbiturates, DMT, etc.) in order to control or self-medicate their volatile feelings—discharging anger, overcoming feelings of emptiness and boredom, overriding painful affects (Masterson & Strodbleck, 1972).

TELESCOPING, CONCOMITANT DISEASE, AND RISK

Nonspecific Concomitant Disease

Research on the association between specific concomitant disease mental illnesses and drug abuse disorders, such as the association between

ADHD and stimulant abuse, is far less extensive than research suggesting a general or nonspecific relationship between substance abuse and concurrent psychiatric disorders (Bukstein et al., 1989). Nonspecific concomitant disease manifests itself in one main way: the amplification of the severity of additional symptoms or "problem behaviors." That is, either mental illness or substance abuse disorder taken singly will create substantial risk of the other, with the result that the subsequent onset of either disease, in the presence of the other, then creates an unstable arrangement of positive feedback between two conditions: symptoms will accordingly become more severe and problem behavior more intractable.

Reasoning in this way about the causal interdependence of mental illness and chemical dependency is compatible with the proposition, considered earlier, that it is not specific psychiatric illnesses but the severity of psychiatric symptoms that predicts prognosis, and that both mental illness and substance abuse disorders are affected by "general life problems" in adolescence. Emerging from this research, therefore, is a picture of how disorganized and unstable life circumstances, among adolescents even more so than among adults, create liabilities to drug abuse disorders and to associated psychiatric conditions, and accelerate the disease process associated with any preexisting mental illnesses. These disorders in turn further disorganize and destabilize life circumstances. Coupling the normal adolescent need for empathy to any part of this unstable causal loop suggests the special role of adolescence in telescoping these disorders.

Most in keeping with such an observed general pattern of concomitant disease is the hypothesis that patients with these coexisting disorders are seeking to self-medicate dysphoric subjective states. The psychopharmacological properties of many illicit drugs, according to this familiar hypothesis, override the feelings and moods associated with incipient mental illnesses and likewise regulate unwanted feelings associated with frightening or anxiety-producing status changes. The self-medication hypothesis, as is generally understood, may well eventually be subject to explanatory reproduction in view of specific knowledge of the effects on brain chemistry of ingesting different substances. The specific way ingesting a substance such as cocaine affects the release and reuptake of neurotransmitters in the so-called brain reward system (Olds, 1958; Olds & Milner, 1954), for example, suggests a more general model for how other chemicals change moods, alter affect, and produce behavioral consequences.

These psychopharmacologic hypotheses, moreover, are fully consistent with the object relations perspective advanced above. In object relations theory, the general model for persons seeking to self-medicate themselves is the model of the dependent person whose behavior, driven by psychological deficits, is controlled by the need for continued caregiving—by deficits in the matters referred to earlier as self-esteem and self-control, deficits which predispose such persons to recapitulate caregiving relationships with others. Such persons are chronically predisposed by their psychological wants to search for regulation for themselves in relationships to external structures, whether these external structures are other persons, social groups, habits and practices, or chemical substances. One recognizes such persons by the readiness they display to come under the control of "objects" or processes located in the "foreground" of experience— the place where they find structures capable of triggering powerful biochemical effects that alter moods, change feelings, and directly affect cognition.

The following are descriptions of the differential use of illicit drugs to self medicate various psychiatric conditions.

Choice of Self Medication
in Various Psychiatric Conditions

Anxiety Disorder

High rates of anxiety disorders have regularly been reported among substance abusers, particularly abusers of alcohol (Weiss & Rosenberg, 1985). While retrospective studies typically provide evidence that anxiety symptoms usually precede the onset of substance abuse, the clear case for self-medication on the basis of such evidence sometimes seems confused by the fact that anxiety is also invariable among the symptoms of withdrawal or projected abstinence from substance abuse. Surveys reporting large numbers of adolescents using drugs to "relieve tension" or "to relax" (Johnson & O'Malley, 1986), for example, are unable to separate primary from secondary disorders. Yet for fairly obvious reasons already considered, anxiety is among the most frequently cited features in adolescent self-reports, and drug abuse typically begins during this period. Psychological predispositions that during childhood would not create strong signals of a psychiatric nature tend during adolescence to be amplified by general life problems. Apparently disease-free children are pushed over the edge by these stressors and begin to feel needs to reduce tension or self-medicate. Moreover as Christie and colleagues (1988, p. 97) point out, "The common tendency for adult respondents to pinpoint very early ages, even before adolescence, for the onset of symptoms of anxiety disorders emphasizes the possible continuity of childhood anxiety disorder like separation anxiety, school avoidance and other phobic behaviors, and obsessive-compulsive disorder with similar conditions persisting into adult life.'' The Epidemiologic Catchment Area Program data examined by Christie and others (1988) showed that, among adolescents and young adults, the risk for drug abuse disorders was doubled by the onset of anxiety disorders. Seventy-five percent of their respondents who reported the onset of anxiety disorders before age 20 went on to develop substance abuse disorders.

Schizophrenia

Schizophrenia is a mental illness which often manifests itself in late adolescence or early adulthood. In its early phases, it is often difficult to diagnose inasmuch as overt psychotic symptoms are not evident. It is, however, significant that these individuals often will seek to self medicate as a result of distressing symptoms with mood altering substances, especially the opiates. Bipolar Disorder (Manic Depressive Illness) may also manifest itself in adolescence and substance abuse is not uncommon. The diagnosis is often very difficult and only made in retrospect. It is important to note that there is a general consensus that the incidence of Schizophrenia is one percent of the population world wide and tends to manifest itself in early adolescence or early adulthood. Those adolescents who are suffering from this condition combined with substance abuse or dependence are difficult to diagnose even for the seasoned clinician. This is of primary importance in that the health care professional must be aware that this condition exists, the prevalence of same, and that this condition may be present. To further complicate this differential diagnosis is the fact that hallucinogens, Phencyclidine (PCP, angel dust), cannabis (marijuana) and stimulants including cocaine, ''ice,'' and other amphetamine-like substances may produce a classic paranoid psychosis which is indistinguishable from an acute psychotic episode. To make things even more difficult, it is not unusual that adolescents may be using a myriad of mood altering agents (mixed substance abuse or dependence) which can further cloud the picture. It is important however to note that these individuals need to be stabilized in terms of psychotic symptomolology first, before the coexistence of the two problems can be addressed if, in fact, they are present. At this point, it is also important to note that individuals suffering from borderline personalities, histrionic personalities, and obsessive compulsive personalities may experience micropsychotic episodes and often abuse substances and are a marked challenge to any therapeutic setting and treatment.

Affective Disorder

Until the 1970's, depression in children was not officially recognized in the United States. The study of mood disorders in adolescents as well as children has gained acceptance and it is clear that depression occurs at all ages. Adolescents who suffer from depression will often self-medicate with alcohol with an attempt to attain euphoria, without being aware that it results in further depression. Cocaine and crack cocaine are often used for elevating mood (Daley, Moss, & Campell, 1987). United States psychiatrists often diagnose mood disorders as Attention Deficit Hyperactivity Disorder, Schizophrenia or conduct disorder.

Prevalence of mood disorders indicates 1.8 percent of the population and 4.7 percent in 14-16 year olds are affected. Adolescents with mood disorders are more likely to have an acute onset. Bipolar illness may begin with depression in prepubertal years and shift to mania during puberty, or begin suddenly with a manic psychosis anytime during adolescence (Strober & Carlson, 1982). Approximately 20 percent of adolescents with mood disorders have a history of substance dependence. The diagnosis of Bipolar Disorder if preceded by a history of substance abuse should be deferred until the adolescent has been drug free and/or detoxified. However, the chronology is not always clear and a clinical trial of Lithium or antidepressant may be indicated (De Long & Aldershof, 1987).

One out of three adolescents will admit to suicidal ideation, and five percent will give a history of a past attempt. Frequency of completed suicides increases with age, with 15-19 year olds ten times more likely to commit suicide than their younger counterparts.

Clinical experience indicated that successful treatment includes group therapy, family therapy, individual therapy, social skills training, and concomitant psychopharmacoltherapy. Controlled data in this population is lacking.

Suicide is a specifically high risk. Recent studies of metropolitan teen-age suicide demonstrated that common precipitating factors were discipline and relationship disruption with a peer. Fifteen percent fulfilled criteria for a major depressive episode, 45 percent had a history of aggressive behavior and 40 percent had been intoxicated with mood altering substances at least three times, difficulties at school, or warned by peers or parents regarding alcohol and illicit drug use (Pfeffer, 1986).

Average length of depression in adolescents is eight months, manic episodes three to four months. Once a good response to appropriate medication has been reached, it should be continued for four to six months.

Conduct Disorder

Anti-social personality disorder has been identified as the primary coexisting diagnosis in male adult substance abusers for many years. However, it is important to note that the use of virtually all mood altering substances result in a criminal activity if only in the purchase of the drug and subsequent contact with a criminal element. Also, the very use of mood altering substances results in conduct such as violent behavior, increased risk taking behavior and general behavioral dysinhibition resulting in deviant behavior. The history of sadistic behavior prior to the use of mood altering substances as well as a history of mixed substance abuse from all four groups of drugs increases the probability of this diagnosis coexisting rather than being the consequence of the substance abuse itself. The personality disorders often associated with substance abuse are narcissistic personality, borderline personality, anti-social personality, and histrionic personality (Short & Strodbeck, 1965).

CLINICAL IMPLICATIONS
FOR DUAL DIAGNOSIS

Opposing Treatment Strategies

Observing persons who have coexisting mental illnesses and substance abuse disorders, psychiatrists and chemical dependence personnel sometimes support opposing treatment strategies. Psychiatrists often emphasize long-term individual therapy, aimed at uncovering conflicts or recapitulating caregiving relationships, based on psychological regression. The rationale for such psychotherapy is long-term: placing the patient in circumstances where he or she might follow a course of psychological growth or healing, eventually enabling the recovery of health, self-esteem, and self-control. Chemical dependence programs, by contrast, emphasize the immediate reversal of patients' regressions and the elimination or control of their dependencies. The rationale for these strategies is that patients must first be detoxified and stabilized psychopharmacologically before an accurate diagnosis of underlying psychological problems can be completed. Many drug-induced symptoms of mental illness – including, in one of Chatlos' (1989) lists, "psychoactive-substance-induced organic mental disorders in DSM-III; intoxication, withdrawal, withdrawal delirium, hallucinosis, delusional disorder, alcohol amnestic syndrome" – prove themselves to be transient in such regimes of detoxification, disappearing within days or weeks of the initiation of abstinence. Others, which do not disappear, usually indicate preexisting psychiatric illnesses. It is these illnesses that should then be amenable to pharmacologic and psychiatric intervention.

Such opposing strategies occasionally work to compromise each other's objectives. Reversing regressive behavior will typically do further psychological injury to the borderline patient, for example, whereas supporting regression in long-term therapy will sometimes deepen patterns of chemical abuse. Similar problems may arise from opposing treatment strategies connected with pharmacological versus behavior modification programs. Just as depriving a schizophrenic patient of antipsychotic medication as part of a regime of chemical detoxification will typically render the patient unmanageable, attempting to treat a chemically-induced psychosis with drugs may worsen the prognosis for subsequent recovery from chemical abuse.

The Primary Illness

With obvious exceptions like those where a preexisting psychosis demands pharmacologic intervention as part of a program for stabilizing chemically dependent patients, the main rule-of-thumb advocated in the dual diagnosis treatment literature has nevertheless been to first detoxify patients before attempting their further evaluation. Gitlow and Peyser (1980), discussing alcohol abuse, speak of chemical dependence in this sense as the "primary illness." Given present knowledge about how drugs can profoundly affect mind and body, they argue, whenever chemical dependence develops in a patient, it becomes the primary illness. "Though the [alcoholic's] illness may begin from quite diverse origins, once the disease of [alcoholism] has been grafted onto this personality structure, it dominates the clinical picture and eventually becomes the major determinant in both choice and efficacy of treatment" (Gitlow & Peyser, 1980; quoted in Chatlos, 1989, p. 191). This argument leads Chatlos (1989), to reason in the light of Engel's (1980, 1977) biopsychosocial disease model, that drug abuse creates "a new illness," one intertwined with preexisting problems "as a result of conditioning of the body and behavior by both drugs and learning effects" (Donovan & Marlatt, 1988). Even removing the drugs leaves behind such conditioned effects on behavior. These conditioned effects — "drug urges or cravings, impulsiveness, paranoia, fearlessness, distrust" — should constitute the focus for treatment programs. Chatlos also draws on the argument presented by Morrison (e.g., Morrison & Smith, 1987) that drug abuse eventually causes a patient to cross what he terms a "biochemical-genetic" line. Once this line is passed, the addicted person is controlled by chemicals and by the processes of acquiring and ingesting them. Such persons, he argues, are wholly dominated by cravings and "urges" which displace logical and rational thought.

When attention does turn toward treatment of dually diagnosed persons, this perspective on the mentally ill chemical abuser is further guided by the biopsychosocial disease model. Of first concern, therefore, is the biological part of whatever disorders present themselves. Only while managing detoxification in a drug-free environment should coexisting disorders be considered. Health care personnel in such circumstances should therefore first be sensitive to drug-induced organic mental disorders that are frequent covariates of abuse and withdrawal, and thereafter to physical illnesses with a potential part in the withdrawal syndrome: "hypo- and hyperthyroidism, seizure disorders, vitamin deficiencies, diabetes, infectious diseases, and heavy mental deficiencies or toxicity," is the list Chatlos (1989, p. 192) presents.

It is only after such evaluation (including any pharmacologic treatment for specific psychiatric conditions like bipolar disorder) that further psychological treatment should proceed. The psychiatric treatment models for adolescent MICA's described in the dual diagnosis literature cover a wide range of approaches, from traditional psychotherapy to variants on 12-step models adapted to inpatient psychiatric settings. Discussions of these variants, within the limits established by available resources, either advocate or are receptive to mixing into treatment individual and group psychotherapy, effective programs for behavior modification, and pharmacotherapy.

Commitments to Abstinence

In dealing with teenagers realistically, numerous programs across the country advocate the development of a primary commitment to abstinence based on some version of the Twelve Steps of AA (Alcoholics Anonymous, 1985). But because, as Chatlos convincingly argues, the primary illness of chemical dependence produces complex and entrenched forms of habituation of the brain and of behavior, managing and sustaining commitments to abstinence is likely to be a difficult process marked by predictable plateaus, resistances, and interruptions:

> A lesson has been learned from treating chemical dependence, that can be applied to other disorders: treating addiction as a primary illness and the roles of a commitment to abstinence. The emphasis is placed on the starting point of a commitment to abstinence, not as the end goal. Starting this way leads to predictable effects. Meaningfully verbalizing this commitment leads to emotional and behavioral

reactions by the patient. These reactions display patterns of behavior demonstrating their specific and individual psychological history. (1989, p. 193)

Significantly, Chatlos and colleagues have found the first five steps of the Twelve-Steps of AA particularly useful in supporting teenagers in their struggles to keep a commitment to abstinence.

Viewed from the point of view, say of Kohutian psychotherapy, such explicitly verbalized commitments are "idealization" — self objects (his "cultural self objects") into which the patient can project and stabilize omnipotence. Such idealized structures begin to establish emotional and cognitive foundations for an effective treatment relationship, i.e., a relationship in which the patient can begin to build the sorts of psychological structure that will eventually enable him or her to diminish dependence on external structures. These foundations rest in dynamics at several levels of functioning: first, they recapitulate the helplessness of the infant in the presence of urges and wants over which it has no control. Second, they thereby configure the patient in relation to both the group and the therapist in caregiving relationships; relationships, on the one hand, in which the group and therapist can serve to mirror the helpless member, and in which, on the other hand, both the group and the therapist can serve as vehicles for idealizing self object transferences. The explicit spiritual formula of the AA Twelve Step Program's first steps is successful in proportion to its ability to elicit from patients their profound wants for strength and direction in the face of what it formulates as their personal weakness and moral corruption. Though this is not Chatlos' point of view, he argues that this adaptation of the AA model "allows [adolescents] to learn a specific technology that provides them with a powerful self-control, which can be used throughout their recovery" (p. 195).

Resistance, Relapse, and Recovery

Interesting psychologically in what Chatlos and his colleagues have discovered in using this treatment model for dealing with dependence, are the ways in which he calls the structures-from-the-past affect relapses from progress along their five-step abbreviation of the 12-step route. By setting up this five-step cognitive-emotional foundation for commitment, they regularly activate sequentially-appearing patterns of resistance to recovery. "These patterns," Chatlos (p. 195) writes, "are referred to as 'structures from the past,' a neutral term that allows discussion by psychoanalytic therapists, self psychologists, developmental psychologists, behaviorist, and learning theorist. These patterns or structures from the past are the result of learned coping patterns, including ego defenses, perceptual and cognitive distortions, and urges."

Treatment typically causes a sequential unfolding of "block to recovery." Part of the dishabituation of the patient, in treatment for chemical dependence no less than in other forms of psychotherapy, are predictable patterns of resistance. Viewed purely from the perspective of treatment for chemical dependence, such resistances are related to well known phenomena of abstinence and withdrawal. More broadly conceived, such blocks to recovery may include "aggressive assaults, overwhelming guilt or shame, depression with hopelessness and suicide attempts, feelings of failure and withdrawal, sexual urges and acting out, binging and purging behavior, and multiple urges that may be acted on or verbalized." Chatlos views these matters as "patterns of relapse," and interprets their appearance not as signals of weakness but as signs of the strength of patients' commitments. Helping patients to understand this through the technique of "reframing"—showing them that they are not relapsing, but predictably resisting recovery—helps to make their resistance comprehensible to them. It also may aid in "identifying specific events in their lives . . . associated with these behaviors."

Recognizing such structures-from-the-past in patterns-of-relapse is what effective psychotherapy is all about: "identifying these structures, recalling the past events in detail, reexperiencing the thought, feelings, and behaviors associated with the event[s], and then acting in the present to produce a different result" (Chatlos, 1989, p.195).

Differential Diagnosis

The differential diagnosis of the MICA patient includes diagnosing if, in fact, the person has a substance abuse or dependence problem, a psychiatric disorder, or both. At times, this diagnosis can definitely be made only after thorough evaluation which may include inpatient treatment and observation. The assessment of the adolescent not only requires a knowledge in the field of mental health and addiction but a knowledge of the developmental stages of adolescence and family dynamics. As a result, the diagnosis or lack thereof is generally a team effort which includes, if possible, a social worker, physician, psychologist, nurse, and the certified addiction counselor. Diagnosis must be made not only on empirical findings but objective findings which at the very least, include an extensive clinical history, physical examination, mental status examination, psychological testing and interview with significant others. Once the diagnosis has been made, the appropriate intervention and an individualized treatment plan must be formed which in this clinician's experience has been most successful when the patient's own goals become the primary aspect of the treatment. Because of a variety of problems and vast differences in adolescence, it must be specific for the individual inasmuch as the expectations of a 14 year old versus those of a 19 year old are substantially different, as are the abilities of a late adolescent who is suffering from schizophrenia and substance dependence compared to those of a 14 year old who has a learning disability or attention deficit disorder.

Group therapy, especially using the Yalom (1985) model, remains the core of effective treatment for most patients with substance abuse disorders.However, the type of group therapy may be dictated by the coexisting psychiatric disorder. Mutual acceptance, and role modeling are important. Confrontation however can be overwhelming for the psychotic individual. Reality testing and immediate feedback as well as positive reinforcement and peer pressure are helpful. Structure, discipline, and limit setting are essential. Learning and exchange of factual information with a constant installation of hope, positive thinking and optimism is necessary. Individual counseling may be necessary given the particular psychiatric disorder, and education in the form of cognitive therapy or concrete instruction, family involvement, introduction to the twelve step program and educating both the adolescent and family about psychotropic medications are essential. It is also important to establish both short and long term treatment goals. Short term goals include sobriety, abstinence, mental health, regular attendance at 12 step meetings, education, compliance with health and doctors' appointments and developing a structured life style.

Pharmacotherapy in the Adolescent MICA

Psychoparmacotherapy usually has a role, and in certain pathological states a crucial role, in the treatment of the mentally ill adolescent. Systematic research, however, on the efficacy of psychoactive drugs for this age group as well as safety is lacking and not available (Campel & Spencer, 1988).

Severity of symptoms, interference with adolescent's development and learning, as well as the reliability of the youngster's support system and family are important determining factors. Pharmacotherapy should never be used as a sole treatment and only in conjunction with psychosocial treatments.

Education regarding medication is important, including benefits versus risks, as well as differentiating between illicit and licit drugs. Polypharmacotherapy should be avoided. Except for rare exceptions, sedatives, hypnotics, and stimulants including the benzodiazepines are contraindicated in the substance dependent person. Phenobarbital may be necessary in seizure disorders, and methylpheridate (Ritalin) in those diagnosed as suffering from ADHD. Lithium and tricyclic antidepressants such as imipramine may be very useful, and even crucial, in recovery from affective disorder.

Anxiety disorder should be addressed by psychosocial treatments including behavioral therapies, and group therapy. Obsessive/compulsive disorder may require chloripramine, and severe panic states psychotropic medication which does not have a mood altering effect assuming that the benefits of same are greater than the risks and accompanied by psychosocial treatment. Neuroleptics in the young must be carefully considered in regard to benefits and long term potential side effects in Schizophrenic patients.

Indications for Inpatient Rehabilitation

1. Strong denial not amenable to previous treatment
2. Too slow an outpatient recovery
3. Individuals who are a danger to themselves or others as a result of their addiction
4. Individuals who have severe psychiatric or ethical problems
5. Individuals who have either no or very weak support systems
6. Patients who request inpatient treatment and in the judgment of the treating staff are motivated to recover, after failure of outpatient treatment (Alterman, Erdlen, La Porte, & Erdlen, 1982).

Treatment Goals

The ideal goals of treatment for the addicted individual during his or her first recovery and which would include initial detoxification are:

1. Breakdown of denial or expressed in a psycho-spiritual way "surrender."
2. Educating the addicted individual about chemical dependence and the disease process.
3. Providing an introduction to group treatment which, of course, includes the utilization of and participation in the self help group

movement (AA and NA as well as others such as the Aids self-help groups if appropriate, Adult Children, etc.).
4. Becoming aware of feelings and handling them.
5. Learning how to ask for help and how to communicate directly and honestly.
6. Involving the family or significant others in treatment (Whitfield, 1984).

Long Term Treatment Goals

Long term treatment goals which may require one to two years are:

1. Ability to express oneself openly and honestly in a socially appropriate manner (assertiveness training).
2. Learning how to enjoy life without chemicals.
3. Beginning family restructuring.
4. Developing specific and long term goals which would include regular attendance and participation in the self help group and 12 step programs, vocational rehabilitation, medical compliance, etc., (Whitfield, 1984).

All who work in the field know that recovery requires a lot of work and a major effort of at least two to three years on the part of the afflicted person.

DISCUSSION AND CONCLUSIONS

The latest NIHM Epidemiological Catchment Area (ECA) study, (1990) has revealed dual diagnosis rates so prevalent that those treating alcohol and drug abusers will no longer be able to avoid addressing mental illness in programs focused on substance dependence and abuse. The study, according to the researchers, indicate that of those who abuse drugs, more than half suffer from a mental illness. Cocaine abusers show mental illness in excess of 76 percent. Also noted is that the cocaine abuser is already one of the most difficult substance abuse problems to treat. The data reflect that 26 percent suffer from affective disorder, 28 percent from anxiety disorders, 18 percent from anti-social personality disorders, and seven percent meet diagnostic criteria for schizophrenia.

Among those suffering from alcoholism, 37 percent have another diagnosable mental disorder. Anxiety disorders were found in 19 percent, anti-social personality disorders in 14 percent, and affective disorders in 13 percent. Conversely, of those who have suffered from a mental illness other than substance abuse or dependence, 29 percent have a history of substance abuse or dependence during their lifetime. According to the earlier ECA studies, 22.5 percent of the U.S. population has suffered from a mental illness.

Of the 8.3 percent of Americans who have suffered from an affective disorder, one-third reported substance abuse or dependence. ECA researchers discovered that mental illness prevalence rates are twice as high as those in substance abuse treatment programs versus substance abusers who have not sought treatment. That is to say, there is about 55 percent accompanying mental illness for those in treatment versus about 24 percent in untreated substance abusers.

The ever increasing evidence of the coexisting conditions which exist in these individuals requires that both disorders must be addressed and explored in order to formulate an appropriate treatment plan and consequent better clinical results. The traditional splitting of treatment for the adolescent MICA is no longer viable and a comprehensive team effort which utilizes the expertise from the various disciplines of the biopsychosocial model is essential. Also those providers treating this population must master skills outside their field of expertise to address the treatment of these adolescents. It is also essential that treatment includes the family and is located in the community of the patient and his or her social-cultural entities. Drug and alcohol free living environments must be made available such as that at Rutgers University (Laitman, 1987) and every effort to treat adolescents in the situation where they will continue to live, rather than isolating them from the network where they live and learn is essential.

NOTES

1. Crime rates are also a function of the number of adolescents aged 14-24 in the general population. The much discussed relationship between the prevalence of drug dependence and the prevalence of crime is therefore in part a cohort effect, though of course there is also an important direct causal relationship between drug use and antisocial behavior as measured in rates of crime.

2. Different statements and expansions of this model, as it applies to attachments, interaction, and social organization, appear in Smith (in press) and, as it applies to interaction and memory, in Smith and Barclay (1990).

REFERENCES

Alcoholics Anonymous. (1985). *Twelve Steps and Twelve Traditions*. New York: Alcoholics Anonymous World Services.

Alterman, A.I., Erdlen, F.R., McLellan, A.T. (1980). Problems drinking in hospitalized schizophrenic patients. *Addictive Behavior, 5*, 273-276.

Alterman, A.I., Erdlen, D.L., La Porte, D.J., & Erdlen, F.R. (1982). Effects of illicit drug use in an inpatient psychiatric population. *Addictive Behaviors*, 7 *(3)*, 231-242.

Bergman, H.C. & Harris, M. (1985). Substance abuse among young adult chronic patients. *Psychological Rehabilitation Journal*, *12*, 43-54.

Blos, P. 91962). *On Adolescence*. Glencoe, IL: Free Press.

Blos, P. (1967). The second individuation process of adolescence. *Psychoanalytic Study of the Child*, *23*, 162-187.

Braught, G., Brakarsh, D., Follingstad, D. (1973). Drug use in adolescents: a review of psychosocial correlates. *Psychological Bulletin*, *79*, 92-106.

Bukstein, O.G., Brent, D.A., & Kaminer, Y. (1989). Comorbidity of substance abuse and other psychiatric disorders in adolescents. *American Journal of Psychiatry*, *146(9)*, 113-1141.

Campel, M., & Spencer, E.K. (1988). Psycho pharmacology in child and adolescent psychiatry: a view of the last five years. *Journal of the Academy of Child Adolescent Psychiatry*, *23(3)*, 269.

Castellani, S., Petrie, W. M., & Ellinwood, E. (1985). Drug-induced psychosis. In Alterman, A.I. (Ed.), *Substance Abuse and Psychopathology*. New York: Plenum.

Caton, C.L.M., Grainick, A., Bender, S., & Simon, R. (1989). Young chronic patients and substance abuse. *Hospital and Community Psychiatry*, *40(10)*, 1037-1040.

Chatlos, J.C. (1989). Adolescent dual diagnosis: A 12-step transformational model. *Journal of Psychoactive Drugs*, *21(2)*, 189-201.

Christie, K., Burke, J.D. Jr., Ragier, D., Rae, D., Boyd, J., & Locke, B. (1988). Epidemiologic evidence for early onset of mental disorder and higher risk of drug abuse in young adults. *American Journal of Psychiatry*, *145*, 971-975.

Christie, K., & Seely, J. (Ed.) (1984). *Working with the Family in Primary Care: a Systemic Approach to Health and Illness*. New York: Praeger.

Cloninger, D.R. (1987). Neurogenetic adaptive mechanisms in alcoholism. *Science*, *236*, 410-416.

Daley, D.C., Moss, H., & Campell, S.S.F. (1987). *Dual Disorders*. Hazelden.

Davis, D.I. (1984). Differences in the use of substances of abuse by psychiatric patients compared with medical and surgical patients. *Journal of Nervous and Mental Disease*, *172*, 654-657.

Davis, K. (1968). Adolescence and the social structure. In Seedman, J. (ed.) *The Adolescent* New York: Holt, Rinehart & Winston.

De Long, G.R., & Adershof, A.L. (1987). Longterm experience with lithium treatment in childhood: correlation with clinical diagnosis. *Journal of the American Academy of Clinical Adolescent Psychiatry*, *36*, 389.

Deykin, E.Y., Levy, J.C., & Wells, V. (1987). Adolescent depression, alcohol, and drug abuse. *American Journal of Public Health*, *77*, 178-182.

Donovan, H. & Marlatt, G.A. (1988). *Assessment of Addictive Behaviors*. New York: Guilford.

Drake, R.E. & Wallach, M. (1989). Substance abuse among the chronically mentally ill. *Hospital and Community Psychiatry, 40(10),* 1041-1046.

Engel, G.L. (1977). The need for a new medical model. *Science, 196,* 129-136.

Fischer, D.E., Halikas, J.A., Baker, J.W. (1975). Frequency and patterns of drug use in psychiatric patients. *Diseases of the Nervous System, 36,* 550-553.

Forno, J.J., Young, R.T., & Levitt, C. (1981). Cocaine abuse—The evolution from cocoa leaves to freebase. *Journal of Drug Education, 11,* 311-315.

Garfinkel, (1987). Adolescent suicide. *Psychiatry Letter, 7.*

Gawin, F.H. & Kleber, H.D. (1984). Cocaine abuse treatment. *Archives of General Psychiatry, 41,* 903-909.

Gitlow, S.E. & Peyser, H.S. (Ed.), (1980). *Alcoholism: A Practical Treatment Guide.* New York: Grune & Stratton.

Graham, P. & Rutter, M. (1985). Adolescent Disorders. In Rutter, M. & Hersov, L. (Eds.) *Child and Adolescent Psychiatry: Modern Approaches.* Oxford: Blackwell Scientific.

Hasin, D.S., Endicott, J., & Lewis, C. (1985). Alcohol and drug use in patients with affective syndromes. *Comprehension Psychiatry, 26,* 283-295.

Johnson, L.D. & O'Malley, P.M. (1986). Why do the nation's students use drugs and alcohol? Self-reported reasons from nine national surveys. *Journal of Drug Issues, 16,* 29-66.

Kernberg, O.F. (1975). *Borderline Conditions and Pathological Narcissism.* New York: Jason Aronson.

Knudsen, E.J. & Treece, C. (1985). Cannabis and neuroleptic agents in schizophrenia. *Acta Psychiatrica Scandinavica, 69,* 162-174.

Kohut, H. (1971). *The Analysis of the Self.* New York: International Universities Press.

Kohut, H. (1977). *The Restoration of Self.* New York: International Universities Press.

Kohut, H. (1984). The self psychological approach to defense and resistance. *How Does Analysis Cure.* Chicago & London: University of Chicago Press.

Laitman, L. (1987). Overview of a university student assistance program. *Journal of American College Health, 36,* 103-108.

Masterson, J., & Strodbleck, P. (1972). *Treatment of the Borderline Adolescent: A Developmental Approach.* New York: John Wiley.

McLellan, A.T., Erdlen, F.R., Erdlin, D.L., & O'Brien, C.P. (1981). Psychological severity and response to alcoholism rehabilitation. *Drug and Alcohol Dependence, 8,* 23-25.

Melges, F.T., & Swartz, M. (1989). Oscillations of attachment in borderline personality disorder. *American Journal of Psychiatry, 146(9),* 1115-1120.

Morrison, M.A., & Smith, Q.T. (1987). Psychiatric issues of adolescent chemical dependence. *Pediatric Clinics of North America, 34(2),* 461-481.

Myers, J.K., Weissman, M.M., Tischler, G.L. (1984). Six months of prevalence of psychiatric disorders in three communities. *Archives of General Psychiatry, 41,* 959-967.

Needle, R. (1986). Interpersonal influences of drug use . . . the role of older siblings, parents, and peers. *International Journal of Addictions, 21,* 739.

Olds, J. (1958). Self stimulation of the brain. *Science, 127,* 315.

Olds, J. & Milner, P. (1954). Positive reinforcement produced by electrical stimulation of the septal area and other regions of the rat brain. *Journal of Comparative Physiological Psychology, 47,* 419.

Parsons, T. (1954). *Essays in Sociological Theory.* Glencoe, IL: Free Press.

Pfeffer, C.R. (1986). *The Suicidal Child.* New York: Guilford.

Price, R.A., Kidd, K.K., & Weissman, M.M. (1987). Early onset (under age 30 years) and panic disorder as markers for etiological homogeneity in major depression. *Archives of General Psychiatry, 44,* 434-440.

Richard, M.L., Liskow, B.I., & Perry, B.J. (1985). Recent psychostimulant use in hospitalized schizophrenics. *Journal of Clinical Psychiatry, 46,* 79-83.

Robins, L.N., Helzer, J.E., & Weissman, M.N., (1984). Lifetime prevalence of specific psychiatric disorders in three sites. *Archives of General Psychiatry, 41,* 949-958.

Rounsaville, B.J., Dolinsky, Z.S., Babor, T.F., & Meyer, R.E. (1987). Psychopathology as a predictor of treatment outcome in alcoholics. *Archives of General Psychiatry, 44,* 505-513.

Rutter, M., Graham, P., & Chadwick, O., (1976). Adolescent turmoil: fact or fiction? *Journal of Child Psychology and Psychiatry, 17,* 35-36.

Rutter, M. (1986). The developmental psychopathology of depression: issues and perspectives. In Rutter, C.E., Izard A., & Read, P.B. (Ed.) *Depression in Young People: Developmental and Clinical Perspectives.* New York: Guilford Press.

Safer, D.J. (1987). Substance abuse by young adult chronic patients. *Hospital and Community Psychiatry, 38,* 511-514.

Schrier, D. (1989). Teenage Suicide. *New Jersey Psychiatric Association Newsletter, (10).*

Schwartz, S.R., & Goldfinger, S.M. (1981). The new chronic patient: clinical characteristics of an emerging subgroup. *Hospital and Community Psychiatry, 32,* 470-474.

Schwartz, I.M. (1989). Hospitalization of adolescents for psychiatric and substance abuse treatment: legal and ethical issues. *Journal of Adolescent Health Care, 10,* 473-478.

Short, J. & Strodtbeck, P. (1965). *Group Process and Delinquency.* Chicago, IL: University of Chicago Press.

Silberman, Charles E. (1978). *Criminal Violence, Criminal Justice.* New York: Random House.

Stanton, M.D. (1979). Family treatment approaches to drug abuse problems. *Family Process, 18,* 251-280.

Stoffelmeyr, B., Benishek, L.A., Humphreys, K., Lee, J.A., & Mavis, B. (1989). Substance abuse prognosis with an additional psychiatric diagnosis: understanding the relationship. *Journal of Psychoactive Drugs, 21(2),* 145-152.

Strober, M., & Carlson, G. (1982). Bipolar illness in adolescents with major depression. *Archives of General Psychiatry, 39,* 549.

Vingelis, E. & Smart, R.G. (1981). Physical dependence on alcohol in youth. In Israel, Y., Glaser, F.B., & Kalant, H., (Ed.) *Recent Advances in Alcohol and Drug Problems.* New York: Plenum.

Washton, A.M. & Tatarsky, A. (1984). Adverse effects of cocaine abuse. *National Institute of Drug Abuse Monograph, 49,* 247-254.

Weiss, G., Heichtman, L., Perlman, T., Hopkins, J., & Wener, A. Hyperactive as young adults. *Archives of General Psychiatry, 36,* 675-681.

Weiss, K.J., & Rosenberg, D.J. (1985). Prevalence of anxiety disorder among alcoholics. *Journal of Clinical Psychiatry, 46,* 3-5.

Weissman, M.M., Wickramaratne, P., & Merikangas, K.R. (1984). Onset of major depression in early adulthood: increased familial loading and specificity. *Archives of General Psychiatry, 41,* 1136-1143.

Wilson, J.Q., & Herrnstein, R.J. (1985). *Crime and Human Nature.* New York: Simon and Schuster.

Wing, J.K. (1978). Social influences on the course of schizophrenia. In Wynne, L.C., Cromwell, R.L., & Matthysse, S. (ed.) *The Nature of Schizophrenia: New Approaches to Research and Treatment.* New York: John Wiley and Sons.

Wolfe, H.L. & Sorenson, J.L. (1989). Dual diagnosis patients in the urban psychiatric emergency room. *Journal of Psychoactive Drugs, 21,* 169-175.

Yalom, I. (1985). *The Therapy and Practice of Group Psychotherapy, 3rd. Ed.,* New York: Basic Books.

Cult and Cult-Like Pathways Out of Adolescent Addiction

Peter L. Myers

Historically, many individuals have sought a path out of pain and confusion within a smaller, structured alternative to society. One subset are adolescents suffering from conditions such as a "stalled" adolescence, chemical dependency, or isolation. Some of these opt to join unconventional groups commonly termed "cult" or "sect," and experience their membership as highly rewarding in the short term. However, such groups may not provide what is sufficient either for meaningful recovery from addiction, or for resolution of developmental issues. Moreover, when membership comes to an end, problems of societal and family reentry are immense.

SECT AND CULT GROUPS

Sectarian or cult groups have traditionally been studied almost exclusively within the sociology of religion (Yinger, 1970; Wilson, 1970). In the past two decades, some sociologists (Wallis, 1975) have described non-religious sects, but the prevailing practice is to consider the non-religious as a curiosity. This author found that formal expansion and utilization of sect theory was indispensable in analysis of certain psychotherapeutic and political groups (Myers 1972, 1973).

A sect or cult may, according to this broadened perspective, be defined as any insular subcultural or subsocietal "bubble" which is:

Peter L. Myers, PhD, directs an addictions counselor training program at Essex County College in Newark, NJ, and a regional consortium of higher education drug prevention programs.

© 1991 by The Haworth Press, Inc. All rights reserved.   *115*

a. deviant from and antagonistic to some area of societal norms and values, proposing an alternative view.
b. self-defined as elite, special, or superior according to some standard.
c. associated with a strict dogma of belief and behavior, which is expressed in ritual and specialized language (jargon).
d. transforming of member identity, often dramatically as in a conversion experience, and demanding of great member commitment.

This combination of traits maintains the "bubble" and prevents individual or group reabsorption into the sociocultural matrix. The sectarian response may occur in mild or full-blown form within the framework of religion, politics, health, "science," psychotherapy, or addictions recovery. In addition to the defining commonalities listed above, other "optional" features may be present to a greater or lesser extent, including:

e. practices to alter states of consciousness, such as use of mind-altering substances, chanting or meditation, intense group experiences that may induce hysterical conversion reaction, hyperventilation, and possession states . . .
f. messianism, as designated in a living person.
g. communal living arrangements.
h. asceticism.
i. millennial and apocalyptic expectation and prediction.
j. paranoid-like hypotheses.

Nuances of theoretical difference between "sect" and "cult" are not within the scope or purpose of this paper. For stylistic ease, the term "cult" will refer hereafter to all such manifestations. Certain variations need to be briefly noted:

a. groups that have evolved into large "established sects," such as the Christian Science religion and, to a lesser extent, the Jehovah's Witnesses.
b. cults that present a conventional face in order to garner contributions or recruits.
c. cult-like milieus that may exist within or in connection with a conventional administrative structure. This especially pertains to psychotherapeutic and recovery programs.
d. changes that may occur in the direction of behavioral or ideological extremes (as happened with Synanon) or, conversely, in reaccomo-

dation with society (examples being the established sects and the formerly radical political groups).

Literature on adolescent cult membership has three main origins:

a. mention within the sociological analysis of cult dynamics (Glock & Bellah, eds., 1974; Wallis, ed., 1975; Zaretsky & Leone, eds., 1974).
b. journalistic accounts of sect life (Stoner & Parke, 1977; Levine, 1974; Appel, 1974).
c. anti-cult books aimed at families of members or potential members of cults, which tend to weigh "brainwashing" factors in recruitment (Ross, 1988; Shupe et al., 1980)

THE "DEVELOPMENTAL LOGJAM" MODEL OF CULT AFFILIATION

The conventional wisdom within much cult literature assumes that some form of developmental issue or conflict is involved in adolescent cult membership. In this section, this approach will be examined through the work of one author, Saul Levine, as he has most clearly focused this issue, and has grounded his analysis in clinical observation made over a long period of time and with a variety of cult groups. The limitations of the approach will be described, leading toward a more comprehensive model.

On the basis of his clinical observations, and with a theoretical set based on developmental theory, Levine (1984) concludes that the formula for cult affiliation includes two factors or groups of factors:

a. A critical period that features a "confluence of unfaced dilemmas in . . . (a) developmental logjam" (p. 41) which he describes as some combination of isolation, boredom, drift, malaise, inability to conceive of a future for themselves, separation problems, meaninglessness, difficulty in achieving intimacy, and dissatisfaction with their own impulsive behaviors. (pp. 28-38). Parenthetically, these problems all fall under the rubric of the term "alienation" (Seeman, 1959), "alienated" being the inevitable modifier of the noun "youth" for several decades.
b. Levine (1984) considers that the second, crucial element in cult affiliation is an accident of geography or opportunity that introduces the subjects to a cult and opens them to interaction with members (p. 42). The joining of a cult offers a detour around these develop-

mental issues, and other emotional benefits, according to this model.

The sample that has been brought to the attention of Levine in his professional work is remarkable in the unexpected "radical departure" from conventional norms, values, and groups made by the adolescents, especially in their disappearance from family life. This sample would seem to exclude those already somewhat withdrawn from conventional lifestyles. The sample is also limited to middle-class families, who have been described as providing much of the membership of cults that have come under observation.

A COMPREHENSIVE MODEL OF CULT CONVERSION AND OTHER PATHWAYS

The "developmental logjam" model of adolescent cult conversion as developed by Levine and others can be incorporated as a subsystem of a much more comprehensive model. Components of this model would, at a minimum, include the following:

"P" (Problem) component, including the "developmental logjam," but also attention deficit disorders and learning disabilities as well as clinical depression, all of which may have contributed to developmental snags, and familial or environmental stressors. Any and all of these predispose some behavioral adaptation.

"S" (Substance abuse) component, which may be related to the above component in a variety of ways:

i. as a consequence of one or more problem stressors.
ii. feeding back to magnify anxiety, low self-esteem, and feelings of powerlessness, with the cognitive interpretation that stress cannot be decreased without chemical anaesthesia.
iii. as a primary disease in its own right.

"C" (Career pathway) component, referring to any of the affiliative adaptations in response to the painful, stressful, or uncomfortable situations of adolescence and/or substance abuse (that is, flowing from the P and S components). These will be delineated below under the sections "Bottoming Out and Converting: Commonalities/Common Pathways" and "Other Structured Pathways for Adolescents." However, suicidal attempts are certainly a more common pathway for adolescents in pain than is the choice of affiliating to a new group.

The development of a substance abusing adaptation to adolescent difficulties, as well as a cult or other radical career adaptation, depends upon several facilitating, targeting, and funneling factors including but not limited to "opportunity" as cited by Levine (1984). Membership in a social network that includes a subset of substance abusers allows a channel into such an adaptation. The spectrum of abusers ranges from experimenters, hangers-on conforming to peer norms or to *perceived* norms, and the problem or pathology-driven users. The latter category contributes to the pool of potential cult recruits, along with the developmentally snagged and all other varieties of suffering adolescents who see their problems as intractable within their current social framework.

Another set of "targeting" factors are values and attitudes of sociocultural groups that predispose attraction to cults or cultlike groups in general, to particular sorts of groups, or to particular sorts of recruitment techniques presented to the subject. Various observers including Levine (1984) have noted that the Eastern-oriented religious cults have tended to attract the middle-class youth. This generalization holds up for many "exotic" and abstract ideological systems such as leftist political sects. In contrast, the poorer, Caucasian youth may be drawn to ideologies that amplify native and nativist sentiments, such as fundamentalist and rightwing formations.

BOTTOMING OUT AND CONVERTING: COMMONALITIES/COMMON PATHWAYS

Rehabilitative sociology has long stated (McHugh, 1966) that the necessary precursor for rehabilitation of an individual was to "disintegrate" the individuals' bonds with others, and their sense of control over social relationships, until they are a helpless atom. While this analysis was meant to apply to institutional climates, it is also a fair description of the state of addiction just prior to attempts at recovery. In addictions counseling terminology, it is said that addicts must "hit bottom" (reach a point where the current adaptation is intolerable) before they enter treatment or a recovery fellowship. Obviously, the severity of addictive disease alone may not impel the addict to make or accept this move, as many drink or drug themselves to death. The threat of incarceration or unemployment often impels the addict to be at least physically present in treatment or mutual aid groups, whereupon denial may be eventually broached. In Alcoholics Anonymous parlance, this is summed up as follows: "Bring the body and the mind will follow."

Recovering addicts often mention the feeling of being totally alone and devastated, with no control over their lives. This is acknowledged in the

First Step of the recovery fellowships, in which the second sentence is "Our lives had become unmanageable." At this point, if the vicissitudes of geography and acquaintance bring the addict to a cult, and if the value system of the addict does not define the cult as a totally alien possibility, this may be the direction of affiliation. That which precedes prior to cult affiliation (or, indeed, prior to any radical behavioral adaptation) may be engendered by any combination of painful factors from which the individual feels there is no exit, and in which the individual feels alone:

a. consequences of substance abuse or addictive disease
b. any or all of the experiences engendered by a "developmental log-jam" in adolescence/young adulthood
c. sudden loss and/or disappointment

Heavy-using adolescent subcultures in an anti-using community are often disaffiliated from the church, educational, recreational, and other institutions. As the adolescent gravitates into such a network, he or she pulls away from these institutions. To the extent that the family is aware of and actively disapproves of the using behavior, some degree of family disaffiliation is also likely, up to and including homelessness. This decoupling from society opens up the possibility of cult or other reaffiliative adaptation.

The emotional state and cognitive set of the "bottoming out" adolescent predisposes a positive apperception of some cult features during early membership. That is, a lessening of the sense of desperation, of the unbearable painful affect occurs, and it is ascribed to the cult experience. Some cult features are viewed positively in the period prior to actual affiliation, while others are not experienced until membership has been achieved. Aggressive recruiting tactics may or may not play a large part in "signing up" the adolescent: in the experience of this writer, some observers have exaggerated the role of "brainwashing" or "love-bombing" (a cult term describing intense affectionate display by recruiters) in their displeasure with the interpretation that the cult may be really attractive to the recruit.

Earlier in the article, the defining characteristics of cults were itemized. The cult provides withdrawal from society at large into an environment that is safe and in which thought and behavioral norms are carefully structured. Many motives to affiliate derive from these aspects:

a. The resolution of ambiguity, ambivalence, and the reduction of anxiety-producing dissonances or the necessities of difficult choices.
b. Predictability and certainty in values and behavioral norms.

c. A manageable, small social universe, as opposed to the chaotic, overwhelming adult world.
d. Regulation of impulsivity which may have resulted in behaviors with which the individual was not comfortable, and which generated guilt and anxiety.
e. Nurturance, a sense of community, a reliable network of intimates and supporters. (Varies by cult type)

The existence of a cult ideology, and the elitist content, may also generate attractors, such as

f. Purpose, direction, identity, and meaning, as opposed to drift, malaise, and meaninglessness.
g. The enhancement of self-esteem via the (self-defined) elite, saved, or special status of members, coupled with the denigration of outgroups and society as a whole.
h. Simple acceptance.

HISTORICAL PERSPECTIVES ON ADDICTIONS AND CULTS

Social and religious movements offering radically new ideas appear throughout history as a quest for order, meaning, and hope in response to disruptive social and cultural change and in response to social and cultural oppression (Cohn, 1961; Lanternari, 1963). A subtype was labeled by Anthony Wallace (1956) with the term "revitalization movement" to refer to a "deliberate, organized, conscious effort by the members of a society to construct a more satisfying culture" (p. 265). Revolutionary messianic, millennial, or personally transformative themes may be stressed in such movements. Native Americans, who experienced all of the conditions cited above, organized quite a few revitalization movements. One of the conditions that they addressed was rampant alcoholism, a result of disruptive deculturation. The founding of a revitalization movement, and the pattern found often among the Native American groups was that the founder, usually in the throes of a dream, trance, vision, or near-death experience, has an intense experience which involves disintegration of aspects of the identity, and a cognitive restructuring or paradigm shift which Wallace (1956) called a "mazeway reformulation," and which one might view as an "auto-conversion" experience. Two major examples are the prophet Handsome Lake, who founded the cult of the same name, and John Rave, founder of the Peyote cult, both of whom were alcoholics. The Peyote Cult has been a pathway out of alcoholism for many Native Americans, unique in that it utilizes a hallucinogenic substance both as a sacrament and as a catalyst for cognitive restructuring.

Movements such as the above, in which the founder had a solitary conversion experience are certainly analogous to the "spiritual experience" undergone by Bill W., founder of Alcoholics Anonymous. Bill W. and Dr. Bob, the first two members of AA, were Caucasian, a stockbroker and physician, respectively, and obviously not part of an oppressed social group. They did, however, experience total disruption to their personal lives and relationships due to alcoholic disease. Madsen (1974) likened AA to a related phenomenon, which he called the "crisis cult." Sadler (1977) responded that one should hesitate to use such terms to describe Western, urban groups. Another approach would be to ask whether Alcoholics Anonymous or Narcotics Anonymous as practiced in socioeconomically deprived and minority communities could be said to fulfill functions of a revitalization movement as well as a folk psychotherapy for recovery. Limited fieldwork suggests that urban, minority Narcotics Anonymous milieus in particular broaden content beyond the sober and drug-free quest to encompass behavioral, emotional, interpersonal, and attitudinal changes necessary to live cooperatively and positively in a drug and crime-infested environment. Thus, it attempts to construct an alternative lifestyle in the manner of a revitalization movement.

OTHER STRUCTURED PATHWAYS FOR ADOLESCENTS

The first sentence of this article alluded to the historical phenomenon of seeking respite within a separate, structured mini-environment. The nunnery and the French Foreign Legion are examples figuring in popular media treatments. In poor and workingclass communities, the military has been a traditional, normative, and upwardly mobile pathway out of malaise or "trouble."

The following case illustrates a structured, yet non-cult pathway out of developmental malaise and substance abuse.[1]

> In a major northeastern city, an unused rail cut is located near an "alternative" public high school ("The Academy"), for those with attendance problems in conventional high schools. During 1989-1990, some Academy students cut classes and assembled here to consume beer and pot, joined by friends truant from other schools or those who had dropped out entirely. The school maintained a stance

of institutional denial regarding student drug use (Myers, 1990). This quasi-group of ten included a subcluster of three:

Billy B., a seventeen year old from the Academy, formerly at Tech, a high-rated special admissions school. He lives with his single, Caucasian mother and never sees his Black father. Billy is not positive about prospects for the future. Although he had favored marijuana and alcohol exclusively, he was being introduced to LSD in the Spring of 1990 by

Rob H., a seventeen year-old Hispanic, also formerly from Tech, out of school and unemployed. He boasted of over thirty "acid trips." His mother, who lacked fluency in English, was in total denial regarding her son's drug use.

Ben M., an eighteen year-old Hispanic attending the Academy, an early stage alcoholic and the child of an alcoholic father. In early 1990 he disapproved of LSD and, paradoxically, was the source of concern from the LSD users for his drunken, near-violent behavior towards his girlfriend at the beach.

A U.S. Navy recruiting station, near the Academy, became another "hangout" area for these three. They signed up to enter the Navy in September 1990. Rob vowed to "get stoned as much as possible" before entering the service.

Two other attendees at The Tracks included Pola P., a sixteen year old Caucasian female with overlooked, mild ADD, and her boyfriend Dan C. Pola progressed in the abuse spectrum throughout the year, gravitating towards the heavy users during periods of instability in her relationship.

In June a relative brought Pola to NA. Although she was by far the youngest attendee at most meetings, she attended enthusiastically for almost four months, while Dan moved to a decidedly antidrug stance as well. Also during the summer, recruitment plans for Billy, Rob, and Ben were stalled as their high school credits were not up to recruitment standards. Ben became both an LSD user as well as a seller of LSD and hashish, leading to an arrest in December, 1990. Rob's usage pattern remained the same, and Billy increasingly sought out drugs over the summer, although he appeared to have ceased during the late Fall. Thus, as the attempt to resolve a developmental snag through a "radical departure" was frustrated, the tendency to progress further into a drug-centered lifestyle was reinforced.

Two individual members of "leftist" political sects at the Academy (Maoist and Trotskyist) had no recruitment success among the students.

As discussed below, these are not "receptor sites" for the motives of the adolescent substance abuser.

CULT TYPES AND THE ADOLESCENT ADDICT

This section will review the varieties of cults existing in American society within approximately the past decade, with emphasis on attraction for the adolescent substance abuser.

I. Political Cults

Revolutionary political ideals and movements attracted young people in large numbers during the 1910's, 1930's and 1960's, acting as a transmission belt to political cults of that time. To the extent that they subscribed to revolutionary purity and asceticism and disapproved of "dissipatory" behavior, New Left potsmoking and acid-tripping was, for some, inhibited as individuals progressed into hard-core ideological milieus. In the conservative climate in existence at the start of the 1990s, as in the 1950s, most unconventional political activity exists in a "cut-off" status so as to encourage a sectarian identity.

The lack of a personal formula for happiness or self-satisfaction, their relatively cool emotional style, and the highly abstract nature of their ideology render the leftist political sect unlikely to attract adolescents or substance abusers. Least popular are "gathered remnants" of pure ideologues such as the Socialist Labor Party and the Maoists (O'Toole, 1975), the many schismatic Trotskyist sectlets (Myers 1972, 1973). Some revolutionary groups, however, manage to "plug into" popular movements such as rent strikes or civil rights struggles (as was common in the 1930's and 1960's for example). Youths looking for a more comprehensive vision than is provided in the immediate struggle may be interested in the group. It would be unreasonable to define such a process as cult recruitment.

Some organizations are cult-like in their core group, but present a "transitional" or reality-oriented face in the form of a front group or participation in some broader arena. Adolescents, including some relatively moderate substance abusers, have been attracted in small numbers by such strategies but seldom maintain their affiliation.

The unique political cult led by Lyndon LaRouche, is noteworthy for rapidly shifting persecutorial and grandiose formulations (Myers, 1988). It is mentioned here due to the attempts to set up front groups which are presented as statewide "AntiDrug Coalitions" as well as a nonexistent national coalition.

The Northwest U.S.A. in particular has spawned some nativistic and extreme rightist groups that have attracted some downwardly mobile working-class youth, almost in a continuum from "skinhead" and "biker" subcultures, but also drawing upon rural White farming communities (i.e., Posse Comitatus, The Order, etc.). Some of these individuals had been drug users who foreswore use when coming under the influence of the ascetic and anti-drug ideology of the far Right.

II. Religious Cults

Religious cults may be subdivided into the following categories:

a. Eastern oriented groups often led by a messianic and prophetic figure born in an Asian nation. Such groups might or might not be normative in an Asian nation, but assume cult form in the context of American society. These include the Hare Krishna (ISCON), which is discussed later, the Guru Rajneesh group which recently disintegrated in Oregon, and the Divine Light Mission of Guru Maharah Ji, recently in schism.

b. Fundamentalist Protestant groups. In the early 1970's there were several "Jesus People" or "Jesus Freak" cults that converted adolescent substance abusers in revivalist style. These ranged from honest fundamentalist sects to those that incorporated cult features that many have found unsavory, such as the Tony and Susan Alamo Foundation, the Church of Bible Understanding, and the Way International.

c. Crypto-Protestant groups including the Children of God, which used flirting and seduction to recruit, and the large Unification Church of Reverend Sun Myung Moon.

d. Spiritist and spiritualist groups, not including Hispanic folk religions such as espiritismo and Santeria. The Church Universal and Triumphant of Elizabeth Claire Prophet (Guru Ma), to give an example of the specificity of appeal, tends to recruit middleclass and middle-aged life-crisis sufferers.

e. "Jewish Christian" amalgams, as, Jews for Jesus, Hebrew Christians.

f. Hasidic Jewish groups. The Lubavitcher branch of Orthodox Hasidic Jewry in Brooklyn are oriented towards conversion of the acculturated and disaffected Jewish population. Some substance abusing adolescents of secular or Reform Jewish families have converted to the Lubavitcher, which has maintained recruitment centers in mobile vans ("Mitzvah Tanks").

g. Flying saucer cults, crypto-religious in nature, which tend to attract an older, eccentric clientele (Buckner, 1965).

Special Focus: The Hare Krishnas

The International Society for Krishna Consciousness or Hare Krishnas, may be the most studied modern cult. Perhaps for that reason, it has been used as an example of cult pathways out of adolescent drug use. There are significant historical problems with adopting this example as a model. The Hare Krishnas were a manifestation of the countercultural trends of the 1960's. Although estimates vary, their peak size was in the area of 5,000, of whom perhaps 500 remain as members (Hubner and Gruson, 1987 pp. 393, 418). They did indeed thrive on recruitment from a drug using subculture, but that "psychedelic" subculture was highly specific to that time and place, as was the syntonicity of Hare Krishna to the counterculture. The psychedelicists held a crypto-mystical ideology of hallucinogen use, and communal non-mainstream lifestyles (Turn On, Tune In, Drop Out). As the hippie experience soured, Haight-Ashbury utopia turning to dystopia and drugs offering disappointment at best in the long run, The Hare Krishnas were almost tailor-made to meet some of the aspirations and needs of the counterculturalists. Their living arrangements were communal, their ideology stressed transcendence of material reality and unity with the cosmos (indeed, that reality is illusion), and the members continued in the position of "drop out" from society.

The Hare Krishna represented a cult alternative to drugs that was a continuation or amplification of the subcultural (in this case, countercultural) system of the drug users. The entire cultural context in which they flourished has vanished, and one cannot utilize the model in the current situation. If the 1990s prove to be a countercultural decade, analogous phenomena might, however, surface once again.

III. Cultism in Psychotherapy and Addictions Treatment

Psychotherapy (as opposed to addictions-oriented) cults are not particularly significant in addictions recovery, and will be identified briefly. These include "therapies" in the service of political cultism, such as the "social therapy" of the New Alliance Party and the "deprogramming" of the LaRouche cult, cults that spun off from mainstream psychology such as the "Upper West Side Sullivanians," cult-like formations in the Human Potential and encounter group movement, and finally Erhard Skills Training (EST) and Primal Scream. Aesthetic Realism and Scientology occupy a borderline between philosophy, religion, and psychotherapy, and space does not allow a consideration of these groupings. The remainder of this section will be devoted to addictions recovery programs and therapies modeled on these efforts.

Peer self-help approaches to recovery from chemical dependency enclose the addict within an intense environment with the group and group processes as healer. Identities undergo radical change, and philosophies are elaborated that radically contrast the alternative pathways of addiction and recovery. Although one hesitates to characterize most self-help formats as cults, their characteristics offer mild parallelisms with those of cults, and may, by any of a number of self-reinforcing cycles, lead in a more cult-like direction. Addictions and mental health professionals must tread a subtle path which recognizes the tremendous successes of self-help groups, yet addresses the needs of clients in adjusting to a world quite different than that in the long-term rehab or fellowship. These tasks must be accomplished without suggesting to the client that the counselor is critical of the setting which has saved the life of the addict; many already perceive the professional as unsympathetic or ignorant of self-help methods. Two major strains within the peer self-help addiction recovery movements will be addressed, the twelve-step fellowships and the "therapeutic community" movement. The latter, although it is more recent, will be considered first.

The term "therapeutic community" originated in social psychiatry, in the 1950's. At that time, it described milieu treatment and patient government approaches in inpatient psychiatric settings. In the 1960's, the term was adopted by addictions rehabilitation programs that are staffed by addict graduates, which accomplish change through intense group sessions featuring behavioral and attitudinal confrontation and emotional catharsis, in addition to a work and status system that modifies behavior. Therapeutic communities of this sort are descended from Synanon in 1958, via Daytop Village in 1965 and Phoenix House in 1967. They overlap a great deal in the rituals, jargon, and concepts employed. Much of the drug rehabilitation effort in the nation is influenced by this subculture. This writer worked and conducted research within these organizations and their non-addict associates (Myers 1972) and observed examples of tendencies towards cultism, as well as movements away from cultism. Subsequent to this research, Synanon, as was widely reported in the press, degenerated into bizarre ritual, paranoia and violence towards critics, and there was criminal prosecution of the founder, Charles Dederich. To many addictions workers, it seems unfair to feature these events prominently when discussing "TCs" (therapeutic communities), and certainly, most of these agencies have grown away from their extreme dogmatism, insularity, and elitism that was found in the 1970's. Other objectionable features of TCs, such as the harsh rituals called learning experiences, have been modified or discarded. Many agencies have learned the necessity of instituting job training and GED programs, and have instituted pathways into employability other than becoming TC counselors, as was often the only option 20 years ago. Out of financial and organizational necessity, many TCs have a nonaddict board of directors, and professional administrators from a variety of backgrounds. Many are best described as therapeutic milieus operating or managed within a conventional agency setting. The milieus vary by the degree to which they are cult-like.

Many self-help groups are modeled after Alcoholics Anonymous, and are referred to as Twelve Step groups or fellowships. After AA, the largest such group is Narcotics Anonymous. It has experienced exponential growth in recent years, which many authors and researchers have overlooked, even omitting NA in descriptions of the fellowships.

There is a vast literature on AA, which has been variously classified as a folk psychotherapy charismatic healing group, a crisis cult, and other designations. NA is more of an open system, ideologically, than AA, and in that sense is less sect-like. This is due to at least two factors: First, the very newness of NA results in the fact that most members have spent a relatively short time in the organization. It hasn't had the opportunity to "ossify." Second, many NA members have been exposed to a variety of treatment philosophies during drug treatment, often influenced by the therapeutic community approach rather than the Twelve Steps. There is an eclectic, sycretic ideological brew in which members blend their belief systems with the philosophy of NA. Addictions counselors need to be sensitive to these idiosyncratic blends.

> In a recovery support group in an urban community college setting, a student, Jeff K., was living at a Salvation Army residence after completing a stay in a rehabilitative setting. He felt very unhappy about the work requirements and other regulations at the residence. Another student, Tom, who was a resident counselor at a halfway house for alcoholics, helped him to find a bed at his facility. Group members were pleased at the outcome. An African-American female student in AA exclaimed "All Praise Be To the Higher Power," and elaborated on her view that reliance on the Higher Power would guarantee success. Another group member, also an AA member, hesitated and then remarked "Well, it was also the teamwork of the

group and our referral network." The female took the spiritual aspects of the 12-step program much further than the other group members, and the male, who was at this point more clinically oriented, was uncomfortable with a totally supernatural causality theory.

In the same college recovery group, Bob A. related to the group that he suffered from sleep disturbances and nightmares about relapsing into drug use. The facilitator stressed the persistence of sleep disturbances for months following detoxification from depressants, as well as the emergence of denied and anesthetized emotions. Dolores C., new to the group, offered the interpretation that a Lower Power (i.e., Satan) was trying to get Jim to drink and drug again. Two other members nodded confirmation. Among some local African-American NA members Satan (pronounced Say*tan*) is a dualistic counterpoint to the Higher Power. Dolores was making her own idiosyncratic (although parallel) blend of ideologies based on her Christian belief system.

The personification of a supernatural entity as responsible for addiction and relapse, instead of the disease concept, does not help clients to develop insight into the behaviors and emotional dynamics that threaten their recovery. The facilitating counselor, a non-addict, was unassertive in offering a contrasting, nonsupernatural hypothesis, for fear of alienating the client population.

Other NA members import elements of orthodox (Sunni) Islamic groups, and two cases were observed of importation into an NA "qualifying" monologue of the popular psychologies of stress-reduction.

As was originally mentioned, a major counseling task is to aid the client to re-enter various aspects of the everyday society. In the case of graduates from therapeutic communities (TCs), re-entry problems include the following:

1. The TC is a very structured environment, in which decisions are made for the client. Similar to the released prisoner, the TC graduate faces "real world" shock in dealing with institutions including the job and the government: Gossip, politics, irrational supervisors and bureaucracy are situations to be negotiated.

2. The TC graduate has had interpersonal matters not only managed but provided with a format for expressing and resolving conflict. In some such agencies, groups are arranged to allow for the voluble confrontation of one who has given offense (a request for this arrangement is known as

"dropping a slip"). Young TC graduates felt that they would burst when treated rudely or with lack of concern in a new job setting.

3. In addition to being habituated to structure, the TC graduate is accustomed to unbridled, even screaming catharsis in group settings. Adolescent members of an outpatient TC setting had negative feedback from neighborhood shopkeepers on whom they practiced their new interpersonal styles. An in-house newsletter contained a spoof about this situation, entitled "The Mad Confronter." The customs of interpersonal interaction in the wider society come to seem pallid and unsatisfactory to the TC member. The client may dismay or alienate former intimates as well. Family and peer readaptation is often strained by the confrontative style as well as tendency to utilize a restricted code (jargon) in speaking.

For the client emerging from either the TC or the Twelve Step formats, conventional therapies may seem odd. The TC client may perceive conventional group therapy members as "cop-outs" or "zombies," while the AA/NA member is unused to an interactive group and tend to re-orient the format into the serial "sharing" ritual. Moreover, the client may also define anger as something to be suppressed ("Turn It Over") because it endangers sobriety, and require orientation to group formats that encourage the communication of resentments among members.

The Self-Made Sectarian in Recovery

A minority of individuals in self-help movements limit their interests and associations exclusively to the movement, and interpret group philosophy in a rigid and dogmatic manner. Thus, they act as sectarians in a context that is not truly sectarian. Other members may interpret this attitude as extending the discipline of early recovery much too far. Individuals of this type are often the Caucasian, old-style, middle-aged recovering alcoholic. Nan Robertson (1988) quoted an A.A. trustee on "rigid and narrow-minded members, particularly old-timers . . . who find it easier to live with black and white than they do with gray." (p.105). This restricted, defended mode extends beyond thought and speech into the emotional repertoire, in which affect is to be put aside. The auto-sectarian is reminiscent of the paradigm presented by Wallace (1985) who found the "preferred defense structure" of the recovering alcoholic to include all-or-nothing thinking, obsessional focusing, and conflict minimization and avoidance (pp. 28-31).

A minor halo effect encompasses those members who chose these individuals as 12-step "sponsors" (guides, mentors, orientors). In a recovery group on a college campus, a member complained that she had begun to chafe under the dogmatism, rigidity, and controlling behavior of her sponsor. Although the group feared that these remarks merely signaled resistance to the recovery process, her examples appeared to validate her reaction.

INSTABILITY OF THE CULT PATHWAY

A. Dually Diagnosed Members of Cults and Self-Help Groups

One limitation of many addictions' self-help formats is the tendency to overlook psychiatric or neurologic disorders, other than addictions, and to ascribe symptoms of such disorders to aspects of addiction or codependency. On two occasions, behavior that was later diagnosed as stemming from a bipolar mood disorder was categorized by AA rehab staff as a "dry drunk," an AA concept referring to the persistence of alcoholic behaviors after drinking has ceased. The narrow categories of dogma can impact negatively upon the plight of adolescent chemical abusers afflicted with Attention Deficit Disorder, who often constitute a subset of the client population in a treatment facility. The therapeutic community makes "responsible behavior" a central tenet, and minor mistakes such as leaving a light on are seized upon to both chastise the miscreant and to publicly ritually reaffirm ideology and group cohesion. Unfortunately, symptoms of ADD include distractibility, inability to concentrate, impulsivity, disorganization, forgetfulness, and failure to complete tasks (Wender, 1987). The chastisement, which ranges among the TCs from a "haircut" or verbal dressing-down to wearing a sign (or, in the case of the light left on, a light bulb), simply demoralizes and lowers self-esteem even more than has been accomplished by years of academic and social failure. The ultimate result will be the premature departure of the client. In turn, the staff will most likely interpret the "split" as an addictive relapse and/or the failure of the client to overcome so-called "junkie attitudes" or refusal "to make an investment to change." Neuropsychiatric concepts and assessment methods have not yet sufficiently penetrated the world of the addictions treatment center, running the risk of a scapegoat role for the ADD or depressed client.

As to psychotic and borderline states, while cults have earned the reputation for being a refuge for eccentrics, severe psychopathology has only been documented for a few varieties, such as the flying saucer cultic milieus (Buckner, 1965; Myers, 1988). Most religious and political cults depend on the stable activity of their members in order to carry out their functions. Cults, while they may redress unhappiness or developmental conflicts, are not designed to cope with severe psychiatric or addictive disease. Members of AA and NA, in fact, occasionally testify to failed attempts at recovery via sects, prior to AA/NA membership. The physically addicted and out-of-control "gamma" alcoholic is at risk for relapse, as is the binging "epsilon" addict. Binge drinkers often imagine themselves "cured" between binges, and may credit cult conversion. In this light, the binging addict whose use is determined by bipolar mood disorder would risk relapse unless the cult had a framework to interpret and manage severe mood swings. The user whose binges are related to buildup of interpersonal tensions and to cultural norms are more likely to be kept in recovery by immersion in the cult social system.

Addict cult members who relapse experience shame and guilt. Attempts are often made to control and eliminate use. The shame, rather than a wish to reaffiliate with former addict peers, precipitates departures.

B. "Six Month Itches"

Doubts and defections that surface after several months to a year of membership have elapsed have a variety of causes.

1. The basic cultural substrate, which seems to have been eliminated during conversion and early resocialization, often survives in a dormant state, as proven by reappearance. At unguarded moments, or at times when cult life seems especially unrewarding, to hear of former peers moving ahead through school and/or into serious relationships may evoke wistful, sad, longing feelings. Holidays are another such moment. Although these feelings may be denied at the time, they are initiating doubt and reevaluation.

2. After cult "rebirth," the first flush of acceptance, love, novelty, conflict-reduction, and excitement inevitably settles down to routine, if not into monotony, boredom, and exhaustion. There is, ultimately, a failure in the expectation of a personal heaven. Moreover, intimate knowledge of members and leaders, who have been idealized and idolized, also often leads to an altered perception.

3. The cult "bubble" in society: While the cult seems to have "sewn up" the hearts and minds of recruits, it still swims against the tide of the majority culture, devoting a great deal of energy in maintaining defenses. Two contradictions in the cult posture that generate difficulty are:

   a. Purity versus accommodation. As a deviant, isolated group, members are torn between the alternatives of purity, isolation and irrelevance on one hand, or accommodation and self-negation on the other, which generate factionalism. Barely afloat in a hostile sea, they can never be free of the anxiety of losing members overboard to family, job, or fatigue. Although this fear is not unreasonable, it often amounts to an oversensitized phobia about dangerous impurity, amplifying factional stress.

b. Failure of prophecy: in addition to personal disappointment in the cult, expectations and claims that were the basis for recruitment also prove unrealistic.

c. Ultimately, dogmatism is often a tedious discipline. Moreover, it becomes clear to some members that failure to recruit can be tied to dogmatic lack of synchrony with cultural styles.

4. Organizational outcomes of cultism: Irrelevance, isolation, failure of prophecy, loss of members, and routinization of charisma require scapegoats, surrogate struggles and meaningful activities. Organizational adaptations commonly seen in cults include:

a. Finding internal scapegoats, further amplifying factionalism and schismatic tendencies, and using factionalism as a substitute battle. This disillusions and drives away those who have no allegiance to combatants, and who find infighting futile, conterproductive, and unpleasant. This disproportionately affects the adolescent member whose personal motives for affiliating are diminished by intramural strife.

b. Cult leadership may whip up artificial crises, sometimes supported by paranoid persecutorial hypotheses. This was the case with the People's Temple, the Aetherius Society, a flying saucer cult (Wallis, 1975), and the U.S. Labor Party of La Rouche (Myers, 1988).

c. "Upping the ante," or intensifying positions, apocalypticism, ecstacy, or militancy. This has some immediate satisfaction but moves so far from normative cultural styles as to drastically reduce recruitment, and increase member stress and burnout. While examples such as the Weather Underground come to mind, therapeutic movements are also vulnerable to this process. At Encounter, Inc., a therapeutic community for adolescent substance abusers in New York City, charismatic and cathartic healing strategies became increasingly dominant. In group therapies, the time-extended or marathon group develops the most intense emotional states. (Casriel & Deitch, 1968). Under conditions of sleep deprivation, group pressure, and expectation, affective intensity can approach an ecstatic, altered state of consciousness, which may be conceptualized as a redemptive, excorcistic rite. In marathons held at Encounter, many were moved to tears or rage for the first time in adult life, or re-lived early traumas. Yet participants reported a let-down effect upon re-emergence into the everyday world, and difficulty in applying or sustaining the feelings and insights gained in the marathon pressure-cooker. There were attempts to diffuse the intensity of the marathon to routine group sessions. One participant reported:

> I never really knew what it meant to scream 'I'm angry' in a group. It became louder and louder and I felt every nerve in my body . . . participating. At the last 'I'm angry,' suddenly, from the pit of my stomach a mass seemed to rise and go right through my body and out of me. It left me feeling light, free, and happy . . . But then a strange thing happened—I felt sad, I felt cheated. I felt that if I had let out one more 'I'm angry' I would have reached the absolute peak of exhilaration.

The hypercathartic norm excluded and even scapegoated those who could not "perform" adequately, which a former member called "cry or die therapy." Some felt exhausted, drained, and discouraged in external relationships. This exacerbated their isolation, and, therefore, the cultlike position of the subculture.

SUGGESTIONS FOR THE CLINICIAN

1. The clinician needs to be alert to the signs of hidden cultism within seemingly conventional religious, political, and therapeutic organizations. Also in this light, there needs to be awareness of the individual blends that may be made of cultural and religious belief with the concepts of healing fellowships.
2. The clinician requires familiarity with ideological principles concerning emotions and behavior held by recovering cult members, which may inhibit the therapeutic processes initiated by the clinician. This applies as well to clients emerging from cultlike therapeutic milieus.
3. The formerly addicted cult member needs exposure to recovery fellowships, which meet the emotional needs for a smaller, caring, and supportive environment, without the negative aspects of cult life. Members of fellowships who have themselves been through cult experiences should be located to sponsor the recovering cult member.
4. Educational and vocational goals need to be stressed early, so as to facilitate societal re-entry.
5. It is not advisable to devalue the cult experience of the recovering client, which will depress the client and/or trigger a defensive reaction. Rather, it may be emphasized that the cult provided important support and respite, enabled emergence from unsatisfactory developmental malaise and substance abuse and brought out important affiliative and emotional needs of the client. Therefore, it was helpful and appropriate to the indi-

vidual at that time. Now, however, it may be time to individuate and explore a variety of affiliations, relationships, and career possibilities.

6. Families of disaffiliating cult members need to be oriented to the need not to engage in recrimination and guilt-mongering behavior about "what you did to us."

7. The clinician needs to address the mental status of the cult member, which may include disorientation, guilt, shame, anxiety, as well as constricted, prejudicial, dualistic and rigid forms of thought. Encouragement of a widening of cultural and recreational interests can facilitate the growth in more flexible modes of cognition. Pre-existing clinical phenomena such as attentional deficits and depression, which may have contributed to developmental "logjams," academic failure, etc., should be identified.

CONCLUSION

Impelled and buffeted by various forces, carried along by opportunity and available channels, adolescents and young adults travel along one tangent, then another. The cult is one of several radical vectors that by "drawing a line in the sand," seems to provide a quantum leap out of unsatisfactory adolescent malaise, often complicated by substance abuse. Sometimes tangential escape routes are necessary so as to make possible the attainment of an eventual goal, which here is recovery and adulthood.

One can identify broad outlines of the forces contributing to the "moral career" of the adolescent client, in order to afford them a non-judgmental perspective on their past and future. Given the rapidly shifting and complex nature of adolescent networks and quasi-groups, as well as the unique etiological "mix" of factors underlying each addictive syndrome, an accurate predictive model is not a realistic goal.

NOTE

1. The case material in the section "Other Structured Pathways for Adolescents" was collected and developed with the assistance of Molly Myers.

REFERENCES

Appel, W. (1983) *Cults in America* New York, Holt, Rinehart, and Winston.
Buckner, H.T. (1965) The flying saucerians: an open door cult. pp. 223-230 in M. Truzzi (Ed.) *Sociology and Everyday Life* Englewood Cliffs, N.J., Prentice-Hall.

Casriel, D., & Deitch, D. (1968) The marathon: Time extended group therapy. *Current Psychiatric Therapies 8* pp. 163-168.

Cohn, N. (1961) *The Pursuit of the Millennium* New York, Harper and Row.

Galanter, M. (1989) *Cults: Faith, Healing, and Coercion* New York, Oxford University Press.

Hobsbawm, E.J. (1959) *Primitive Rebels* New York, W.W. Norton.

Hubner, J. & Gruson, L. (1987) *Monkey On A Stick: Murder, Madness and the Hare Krishnas* New York, Penguin.

Johnson, G. (1976) The Hare Krishna in San Francisco, In C.Y. Glock and R.N. Bellah, (Eds.), *The New Religious Consciousness* Berkeley, The University of California Press.

Judah, J.S. (1980) *Hare Krishna and the Counterculture* Books, Demand, UMI.

La Barre, W. (1962) *They Shall Take Up Serpents* New York, Schocken.

Levine, F. (1974) *The Strange World of the Hare Krishnas* Greenwich, Fawcett.

Levine, S. (1984) *Radical Departures: Desperate Detours To Growing Up* New York, Harcourt, Brace, Jovanovich.

Lewis, I.M. (1971) *Ecstatic Religion* Harmondsworth, Penguin.

Madsen, W. (1974) Alcoholics Anonymous as a crisis cult, *In Alcohol Health and Research World* Spring 1974.

McHugh, P. (1966) Social disintegration as a requisite of resocialization, *In Social Forces* XVIV, March 1966, pp.355-365.

Myers, P.L. (1972) *"Going Through the Concept"*: Therapeutic Sects In the 1960's Doctoral dissertation, New York University, Department of Anthropology, October 1972 (Dissertation Abstracts International, Volume XXXIII. November 11, 1983).

Myers, P.L. (1973) Therapeutic and political sects. Presented to 72nd Annual Meeting of the American Anthropological Association, New Orleans, November 30, 1973.

Myers, P.L. (1988) Paranoid pseudocommunity beliefs in a sect milieu. *Social Psychiatry and Psychiatric Epidemiology 23*, pp. 252-255.

Myers, P.L. (1990) Sources and configurations of institutional denial. *Employee Assistance Quarterly 5*(3).

O'Toole, R. (1975) Sectarianism in Politics: Case Studies of Marxists and De-Leonists. In R.Wallis (Ed.) *Sectarianism* New York, John Wiley and Sons.

Robinson, N. (1988) *Getting Better: Inside Alcoholism Anonymous* New York, William Morrow and Company.

Ross, J.C. and Langone, M.D. (1988) *Cults: What Parents Should Know*, New York, Lyle Stuart.

Sadler, P.O. (1977) The 'crisis cult' as a voluntary association: an interactional approach to Alcoholics Anonymous.

Seeman, Melvin (1959) On the meaning of alienation. *American Sociological Review*, Vol. 24, December 1959, pp.783-791.

Stoner, C., and Parke, J.A. (1979) *All God's Children*, Harmondsworth Penguin.

Wallace, A. (1956) Revitalization movements, *American Anthropologist 58*, pp. 264-281.

Wallace, J. (1985) Working with the preferred defense structure of the recovering alcoholic. In S. Zimberg, J. Wallace, and S.B. Blume, (Eds.) *Practical Approaches to Alcoholism Psychotherapy* New York, Plenum.

Wallis, R. (1975) The Aetherius Society: A case study in the formation of a mystagogic congregation. In R. Wallis (Ed.), *Sectarianism* New York, John Wiley and Sons.

Wender, P.H. (1987) *The Hyperactive Child, Adolescent, and Adult* New York, Oxford University Press.

Wilson, B.R. (1970) *Religious Sects* New York, McGraw-Hill.

Yinger, J.M. (1970) *The Scientific Study of Religion* New York, MacMillan.

Zaretsky, I.I. & Leone, P. (1974) *Religious Movements in Contemporary America* Princeton, Princeton University Press.

For Product Safety Concerns and Information please contact our EU
representative GPSR@taylorandfrancis.com Taylor & Francis Verlag GmbH,
Kaufingerstraße 24, 80331 München, Germany

Batch number: 08153776

Printed by Printforce, the Netherlands